Sunset
Container Gardening

By the Editors of Sunset Books and Sunset Magazine

Colorful containers of lobelia, star jasmine (*Trachelospermum jasminoides*), violas, and geraniums (*Pelargonium*) lavish bloom and greenery in a quiet corner. Design: Kawasaki/ Theilacker & Associates.

Lane Publishing Co. • Menlo Park, California

Gardening simplified

Whether you do your gardening on an apartment deck, on a typical suburban lot, or on five acres of countryside, containers not only simplify it, but also make it portable, versatile, and almost instantly rewarding.

At Sunset, we've developed expertise in container gardening over decades of research. In this fourth edition of one of our most popular books, we guide you through all the basics of this simple method of growing plants, illustrating all aspects with photography and detailed drawings. Come join us in the outdoor pleasures of cultivating favorite plants in containers.

For carefully checking our manuscript, our special thanks go to Bob Cowden, Philip Edinger, Michael MacCaskey, and William L. Nelson. We also thank Rebecca La Brum for her thorough and sensitive editing.

For their generous assistance in finding examples of container gardening to photograph, we thank Robert Duranleau, East Bay Nursery, James Kalken (Kawasaki/Theilacker), Les Cadeaux, Roger Reynolds Nursery, Scotty Scott (Neel's Nursery), Carol Shuler, The Tree Farm, Van Winden's Nursery, Patricia K. Verbeek and E. Scot Lee (Homescape Designs), and Wildewood Gardens.

Coordinating Editor:
Maureen Zimmerman

Research & Text:
A. Cort Sinnes

Contributing Editor:
Susan Warton

Design:
Roger Flanagan

Illustrations:
Sally Shimizu

Photo Stylist:
JoAnn Masaoka

Splashes of pink bloom cascade from clustered hybrid fuchsias, set in containers raised to varied heights.

Photographers

Glenn Christiansen: 37, 46, 68. **Derek Fell:** 32. **Jerry Fredrick:** 48. **Dorothy Krell:** 4, 13 left, 22 left, 24 top, 26 bottom, 41. **Ells Marugg:** 3 center left, 5 top, 8, 9 bottom, 14 top and bottom, 17 right, 22 bottom, 29 left, 33, 36, 38 right, 40, 47, 54, 63, 71, 72, 80. **Jack McDowell:** 3 center right, 16 bottom, 17 left, 18 bottom, 24 bottom, 26 top left, 29 right, 34, 35, 45, 49, 58, 65, 79. **Don Normark:** 25, 50 right. **Muriel Orans & Arthur Norman Orans:** 15, 57, 61. **Norman A. Plate:** 2, 23, 28, 30, 43, 67. **Victor Reiter:** 39. **Bill Ross:** 21 right, 31. **David Stubbs:** 50 left. **Michael Thompson:** 62. **Verna Van de Water:** 3 right. **Darrow M. Watt:** 18 top, 42, 44 left. **Tom Wyatt:** 1, 3 left, 5 bottom, 6, 7, 9 top, 10, 11, 12, 13 right, 14 left, 16 left and top, 19, 20, 21 left, 22 top, 26 top right, 27, 38 left, 44 right, 51, 52, 53, 55, 56, 59, 60, 64, 66, 69, 70, 73, 74, 75, 76, 77, 78.

Cover: Encircling patio chairs with cheerful color, container-grown annuals, perennials, and trees create an inviting outdoor setting. Photograph by Tom Wyatt. Photo styling by JoAnn Masaoka. Cover design by Naganuma Design & Direction.

Editor, Sunset Books: David E. Clark

First printing October 1984

Contents

Landscaping with containers

Vivid colors of marigolds (*Tagetes*) and geraniums (*Pelargonium*) glow against sparkling view and sun-drenched deck. Design: Michael Westgard.

Place just one pot of bright red geraniums on your window sill, door step, patio, or front walk, and you'll immediately create an eye-catching garden in miniature.

And many a full-scale container landscape begins just that simply. Soon the magic of the first potted plant inspires you to collect a few more . . . and then a few more. You discover a fascinating variety of color, form, size, and scent. You find plants that cascade elegantly from hanging pots—or that splash a formerly barren patio with joyful colors. You gather container plants that, when massed in a cluster, compose a rich tapestry with their foliage.

However you first set up a container landscape, you can redesign it at any time, since potted plants are obligingly portable. Some gardeners, for example, feature a show of bulbs in spring, followed by the paint-box colors of summertime annuals. Many people create a temporary container landscape for one special occasion, such as a party or wedding.

We open this book with a photographic garden tour of exciting ideas for container landscapes at specific points around the home—decks, patios, rooftop gardens, windows, entryways, pool areas, and walkways. Here is special-effect inspiration, too: raised beds (built-in plant containers) and hanging wire baskets (moss-and-flower extravaganzas).

As you take this tour, you'll see breathtaking plantings in plain or fancy tubs and hanging pots, in dazzling sunlight or refreshing shade. You'll see brilliant blooms, some in mixed bouquets, and stately, formal foliage. Most of the great variety of plants in these photographs are described in the alphabetical listings between pages 30 and 81.

Decks, patios & rooftops

Like an empty stage just waiting for your theatrical direction, a deck, patio, or rooftop can display container plants with especially stunning drama.

Container plants make natural accessories to these outdoor living spaces—which also, in most cases, cannot support any other kind of gardening.

Almost anything goes in stage-dressing with plants, from a small tabletop collection of succulents to grand, showy trees in half barrels. Tubbed or airborne mixed bouquets (see pages 24 to 26), brimming with vivid colors, can turn your next patio entertainment into an award-winning performance. As in any container landscaping, rearrangement is easy—whenever whim, special event, or season calls for a change of scene.

To protect your "stage" from stains and possible water damage, be sure to raise up containers or use saucers under them (see page 83).

Colorful contrast

Brightening as well as softening their wooden surroundings, geraniums (*Pelargonium*) and lobelia cluster in pots along deck edge. Special gravel area drains water safely, humidifying plants without staining deck. Design: Wallace K. Huntington.

Clean and bright: White

White lends a clean, serene look all its own—and sometimes glows even more vibrantly than the most vivid flower color. Here, pots of impatiens repeat the white of patio furniture and door trim. Design: Robert Chittock and Berrisford/Moll.

Stage dressing

Coral-blossomed dwarf oleanders (*Nerium oleander*) and tall, burnished jugs line up beneath painting in this handsome patio display.

Cheery surroundings

Billowing so abundantly that they conceal containers from view, flowers and foliage soften austere look of wood house and deck. Bright bouquets include red and pink geraniums (*Pelargonium*), hot pink verbena, and orange impatiens, with a Hollywood juniper in the background. Extra color comes from lavender lobelia, orange butterfly flower (*Schizanthus pinnatus*), marguerites (*Chrysanthemum frutescens*), yellow marigolds (*Tagetes*), blue daisylike *Felicia amelloides*, and fuchsias. Design: R. David Adams Associates, Inc.

Floral fiesta

Bright floral color encircles this Spanish-style patio, blazing from containers of red and pink geraniums (*Pelargonium*) and golden shrub daisies (*Euryops*), and lavender violas planted with butterfly flower (*Schizanthus pinnatus*). Sweet peas (*Lathyrus odoratus*) flank fireplace, and pink cyclamen adorns its mantelpiece. Design: Lew Whitney of Rogers Gardens.

Desert design

Rising gracefully against an adobe column, wiry ocotillo (*Fouquieria splendens*) resembles modern sculpture in its simple clay tub. Its desert garden companions are (left) magenta bougainvillea with asparagus fern and (right) stapelia.

An island of color

Creating an island of color in brick courtyard, containers offer gardener an ever-changing variety of flowers. These pots hold foxglove (*Digitalis*), lobelia, dahlias, verbena, marigolds (*Tagetes*), petunias, cosmos, asters , and geraniums (*Pelargonium*). Hosing down bricks raises humidity for plants.

Tranquility in the treetops

Serenely secluded from the hustle-bustle of streets below, this rooftop container garden includes India hawthorn (*Raphiolepis indica*), pink azaleas (*Rhododendron*), yellow orange marigolds (*Tagetes*), gray-green-leafed pittosporum, and a tall New Zealand laurel (*Corynocarpus laevigata*). Design: Fry & Stone Associates. Architect: John E. MacAllister.

Urbane formality

Elegant penthouse garden gladdens the eye with red, white, and blue combination of petunias, sweet alyssum (*Lobularia maritima*), bachelor's button (*Centaurea cyanus*), and lobelia. Other containers feature trimmed boxwood (*Buxus*), as well as trained ivy (*Hedera*) and privet (*Ligustrum*). Planter boxes roll on casters for easy rearranging.

Poolside plantings

Its cool, crystal-blue surface sparkling in the sun, a swimming pool attracts like nothing else in hot summer weather. But all that blue can also look harsh under brilliant light, especially when surrounded by concrete. Pools need the decorative help of a colorful chaise, a bright patio umbrella, or—you guessed it—container-grown plants.

Even if your pool is actually a hot tub, a fish pond, or just a birdbath, the luxuriance of container-grown bloom and foliage will greatly enhance its appeal. (For a true water garden, with aquatic plants growing right in a tranquil pool, see suggestions on page 45.)

Ferns, shrubs, and blooming annuals and perennials all look lovely in poolside containers. Obviously, though, you'll want to avoid anything with thorns or prickly foliage. Avoid the following plants, too, since they appeal strongly to bees: cotoneaster, English lavender (*Lavandula angustifolia*), escallonia, privet (*Ligustrum*), rosemary, thyme, and wisteria.

Check with nursery personnel to make sure that the foliage of plants you choose won't suffer when dampened. If you do use such plants, protect them from splashes by moving containers away from the water's edge when the pool is in use.

Also let the nursery staff guide you on choosing plants that won't drop fine debris, which could damage a swimming pool's filter. Larger litter (large fallen leaves, for example) won't endanger the filter, but will still cause extra clean-up work.

A number of practical and colorful pool-area possibilities are shown on these two pages. Look through the individual plant entries between pages 30 and 81 for more good candidates, such as these: India hawthorn (*Raphiolepis indica*), lily-of-the-Nile (*Agapanthus*), kaffir lily (*Clivia miniata*), and Japanese aralia (*Fatsia japonica*).

Sylvan symmetry

Twin clay basins displaying cyclamen and maidenhair fern (*Adiantum*) bring cool, sylvan softness to an elegant garden fountain. Design: Rogers Gardens, Brian Benham Landscape.

Poolside bouquet

A brilliant medley of colors, container-grown annuals create pretty bouquet effect at edge of free-form pool. They include floss flower (*Ageratum*), sweet alyssum (*Lobularia maritima*), pansies (*Viola*), and snapdragons (*Antirrhinum majus*).
Design: Don Craig.

Troupe of dancers

Cheerful tubbed plants line up like dancers across a stage as they brighten a stark poolside wall. Dwarf citrus trees, with miniature violas (sometimes called Johnny-jump-ups) at their bases, alternate with double hybrid pink tulips.

Greening the garden path

In today's hurry-up world, there's special appeal in a garden path. Its flowers and foliage seem to invite us to slow down to a gentle strolling pace—even to stop here and there to savor their beauty.

Whether your path wanders through the garden, ambles up a flight of steps, or takes a short, straight route to the front door, plants in containers can enhance every step of the way.

What if you want to create a path where you don't already have one? You can make an instant walkway with container plants—just line up planter boxes or pots in parallel rows. This is an especially effective way to direct traffic at a large outdoor party.

Often serving both functional and decorative purposes at the same time, container plants bring a bright new look to any garden walk or flight of steps. They add just the right finishing touch and note of warm welcome.

You can decorate your walkway with almost any plants you please, provided they can thrive where you place them and won't intrude upon traffic. Your taste may call for stately stands of cypress—or a flood of brilliant zinnias. Either touch of nature will bring obvious visual enrichment to the walk's masonry or brickwork, as well as to the lucky passerby.

Some gardeners set out container-grown plants in formal borders along each side of a path. Others display a casual cluster where the pathway curves—or a pair of "sentinel" shrubs flanking the top of garden steps. Many more landscaping ideas for walks and steps appear on these three pages.

Besides adding romance and beauty, versatile container-grown plants perform practical services along paths and garden steps. Marching along each side, they give strong definition, as if pointing the way. When holding bright, noticeable blooms like the white marguerites shown on the facing page, containers can double as a safety barrier along an edge where people might stumble. And tall, thick foliage from container-grown subjects such as bamboo (see page 14) borders a path (or other paved area), provides privacy, and screens out harsh wind and sunlight.

A leafy welcome

Like a welcoming committee at the foot of stone steps, clipped English laurel (*Prunus laurocerasus*) shares pots with lustrous spills of ivy (*Hedera*). Bright Transvaal daisies (*Gerbera jamesonii*), at right, add a splash of warm color.
Design: Michael Westgard.

Pathway strewn with bloom

Brighten the front walk with pots of blossoming plants—such as these combinations of pink bedding begonias with star jasmine (*Trachelospermum jasminoides*). Asparagus ferns in hanging pots above add soft clouds of green. Design: The Peridian Group.

Crisp white boundaries

Standing in orderly rows, Spanish pots of white long-stemmed marguerites (*Chrysanthemum frutescens*) visually separate garden levels. Design: W. David Poot.

Landscaping with containers 13

Woodsy tranquility

Leafy cascades from Katsura tree (*Cercidiphyllum japonicum*), Japanese maples (*Acer palmatum*), mugho pine (*Pinus mugo mugo*), and cedar transform secluded side of house into sun-dappled forest glade.

Lighting the way

Tubs of dwarf white marguerites (*Chrysanthemum frutescens*) glow in dappled sunlight with as warm a welcome as lantern beams at night—and offer bright contrast to bricks below. Red geraniums (*Pelargonium*) in pot above add vivid accent. Design: Brian Benham and Brent Jamison Landscape.

All in a row

Line-up of graceful, thick-foliaged golden bamboo creates privacy, also buffers wind and sun. Growing bamboo in half barrels or other large containers prevents invasive types from spreading, often a problem in the open garden.

Raised beds: Containers that stay put

Like jewels in a perfect setting, annuals glow with color in trim brick raised beds. Planting includes nemesia, stock (*Matthiola incana*), sweet alyssum (*Lobularia maritima*), and lobelia.

Attractive and easy to use, raised beds have become a widely popular method of growing flowers, vegetables, small trees, and other plants. Essentially just an open-bottomed planter box, a raised bed allows many of the advantages of container gardening.

Like containers, raised beds offer a tidy solution to the problems of crowded garden space and poor native soil. They also provide a simple means of cultivating plants with special soil needs—such as acid-loving azaleas and rhododendrons.

Because a raised bed lifts plants slightly, as a container does, it often displays them more effectively than a ground-level bed. The added height also eases weeding, raking, hoeing, and other chores—making gardening a bit easier on the back.

Raised beds can be more than just planters. The framing supplies support for built-in garden seating—great for summer parties. And when designed in a narrow width and situated, perhaps, along a patio edge, the bed can double as a low dividing wall.

For eager gardeners, a raised bed offers yet another bonus: its soil warms up earlier in spring than the open ground of the garden, so you can start favorite annuals and vegetables that much sooner.

The one obvious difference between a raised bed and a container is that the bed usually becomes a permanent garden fixture. To avoid future frustration, choose its location very carefully. Design in advance what you'll grow in the bed, and estimate how much space these plantings will require. Also consider sunlight needs.

Build your raised bed to whatever dimensions suit your purposes—from a few square feet to several hundred. Experienced raised-bed gardeners suggest planning a width that measures just under twice your arm's length. This way, you'll be able to reach the bed's center from either side and won't have to step directly on its soil when weeding, spraying, or harvesting.

All types of rot and insect-resistant lumber, from wooden stakes to railroad ties, will furnish adequate sides. For a more permanent structure, you may prefer to use masonry—brick, stone, or concrete, for example. (See drawings below.)

Once its sides are installed, a raised bed is ready to fill. Just as you fill a container with potting soil mix, you fill a raised bed with soil that's heavily amended with organic matter. For best results, use a mix that's about half garden loam (see page 95) and half organic materials such as peat moss, nitrogen-fortified sawdust, or compost.

Unless you take steps to mix the new, amended soil with existing soil, the ground beneath the bed may form an impenetrable barrier—a danger to whatever you plant.

When one type of soil lies over another type, water movement across the dividing line (the "interface") slows down or even stops completely. As this happens, the top soil layer stops draining properly; and when it does eventually dry out, water can't move upward by capillary action. As for your plants, if their roots don't drown first, they may die of thirst.

It's easy to prevent such a barrier from forming, though. Rather than adding the new, amended soil in a single, solid layer, you thoroughly mix half of it into the existing ground, by spading or rotary tilling. Then add more new soil until the desired bed level is attained; once again, mix thoroughly.

Three ways to build a raised bed

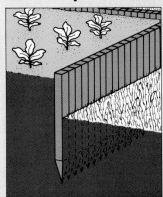

Wooden stakes can be driven into ground in a row. Embed them in a concrete footing for more permanent raised bed.

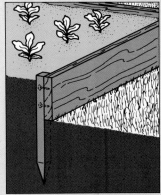

Planks of unsurfaced redwood or cedar make durable raised beds. Use carriage bolts to fasten planks to stakes or posts.

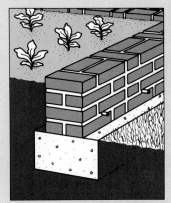

Brick, stone, or concrete makes lasting raised bed. (Pipes are for drainage.) Choose material to complement house construction.

First impressions

To create a glowing first impression of your home, to welcome guests, to celebrate the season—nothing dresses up an entryway quite as effectively as container plants. Even one, standing by the door or trailing elegantly from an overhang, can make all the difference between drab and dramatic.

Along with their welcoming touch, tall or thick plantings give you more privacy from the street. And you can select plants specifically to disguise or enhance architectural features—perhaps to accent the color of your house.

Rotate your display with the seasons, if you wish—blooming bulbs through springtime, a glittering tubbed tree at Christmas. Or, establish a year-round "welcoming committee" at the entryway.

Springtime greetings

Portable pots nestled in lush English ivy (*Hedera helix*—also in pots) dress up front entry for spring. Blooming beauties include pink Martha Washington geraniums (*Pelargonium*), white azaleas (*Rhododendron*), white cyclamen, red tulips, and yellow and white primroses (*Primula*). Design: Azela and Bill Harris.

Formal symmetry

Standing like foliaged sentries at the door, two English ivies (*Hedera helix*) trained up wire supports reflect formal style of house in their symmetrical arrangement. Clustered pots of pink chrysanthemums flank each ivy; small basket of ivy and pink cyclamen on door adds an elegant finishing touch.
Design: Flegel's Home Furnishings, Inc. and Les Cadeaux.

A big, blooming welcome

This colorful, virtually vertical container garden serves two functions—it welcomes guests warmly, yet also partially screens house from street. Hanging bouquets include pink begonias (some accented with verbena), fuchsias, and English primroses (*Primula polyantha*). Tubs of white double marguerites (*Chrysanthemum frutescens*) and golden shrub daisies (*Euryops*) stand at street level. Design: Lew Whitney of Rogers Gardens.

Arching in welcome

With its blossoms up close to eye level, graceful hydrangea lends elegant seasonal trim to front door. Lacy foliage of Japanese maple (*Acer palmatum*) adds leafy contrast to bare-trunked standard.

Entry versatility

Clustered informally near entry, collection of assorted favorite plants can be changed to suit the season. A small standard azalea (*Rhododendron*) shares its tub with cascading lobelia; a variety of ferns and two begonias (one in basket above, the other in pot below) complete the inviting scene.

Landscaping with containers   **17**

Window dressings

Just as shutters and curtains dress up a window, potted plants also brighten its view from both indoors and out. A bold splash of flower color or cascade of leafy green makes even the plainest window look invitingly fresh.

Europeans have appreciated window gardening for generations. Travelers to Europe often come home entranced by such sights as cheery red geraniums spilling from an Alpine window box, or vivid bougainvillea mounding over a filigree Spanish balcony. Inevitably, such window dressings have captured interest in the United States as well.

For apartment and townhouse-dwellers, a window box may offer the only patch of garden possible, whether it holds herbs for the kitchen or multicolored marigolds. But even if you don't live high above a city street, you can still enliven your windows with plants—at whatever level suits you.

A planted window box makes a heavy load, especially after watering, so be sure to anchor it to the house studs with stout supports (lag screws or bolts). If you build your own box, make it at least 9 inches deep, and use lumber that's at least 1 inch thick.

Unless placed on a north-facing wall, a window box often receives fairly intense sunlight during part of the day. And if box or house is painted a dark color, the soil will absorb more heat than usual. Choose sun-loving plants for such situations, and count on daily watering in warm weather.

On these two pages, we show some imaginative alternatives to the traditional window box. A wide ledge lined with potted plants creates the same showy effect, but makes it easier to change pots or to bring them indoors for watering or fertilizing. Planter boxes placed at ground level, under windows, look as dressy as the real thing—like window-ledge displays, they don't require attaching a heavy container to your house.

Finishing touches

A window treatment for the outside of the house, white azaleas (*Rhododendron*) in mock window boxes dress up Victorian frames above them. Trailing English ivy (*Hedera helix*) shares decorative clay planters. Design: Flegel's Home Furnishings, Inc.

Splash on some color

Bold splashes of window-box color—salmon pink, white, and red—accent elegant lines of a plain gray house. Petunias will keep up the show all summer long. Design: James McDonald and Associates.

Floral harmony

Pink impatiens trails over decoratively tiled window ledge; violas, lobelia, and azalea (*Rhododendron*) in harmonizing hues cluster below. Design: Kawasaki/Theilacker Assoc.

Old World charm

As pretty as a picture of Provence, pots of orange and lavender violas feast the eyes. Parting from European tradition, these plants sit atop window ledge (tiled for protection). Design: Kathy Yandell of Inner Gardens Colorscaping.

Gardens in the air

Something spectacular often happens when you lift a plant high in the air. Even those that look sedate on the ground can turn quite acrobatic when suspended in midair and gently stirred by breezes. And some plants— *Camellia sasanqua*, for example—may even change their direction of growth, trailing gracefully downward instead of growing upward.

For a truly showy aerial circus, try pots of fuchsia and brilliant vines such as bougainvillea and lantana.

Hanging a plant brings it close to eye level, so you can more easily enjoy every detail of flowers and foliage. And if you hang the plant in just the right spot, it will double its service by blocking an unwelcome view or screening strong sunlight.

Trailing plants such as vines (see pages 51 to 53) are traditional favorites for hanging containers. But other types have equal aerial appeal; for example, the dramatic foliage of certain succulents can look like fascinating sculpture when displayed up high.

Garden centers carry pots and harnesses designed specifically for hanging up plants. You'll also need heavy hooks and supports stout enough to bear the weight of planted containers just after watering. On page 87, you'll find directions for suspending containers, plus illustrations of several popular types. Plan locations for your aerial pots with care, so you can avoid bumps on the head later on.

Exposed on all sides to sun and wind, hanging plants tend to dry out quickly; you may need to water them daily in hot weather. To promote rich, attractive growth, it's best to fertilize weekly during the spring-through-summer growing season. Use a complete liquid fertilizer, diluted to one-quarter the recommended monthly amount.

On stage: floral acrobats

Looking like acrobats taking a bow, colorful yellow, white, and magenta English primroses (*Primula polyantha*) alternate with tumbling asparagus ferns above a Spanish-style balcony. Chorus of fairy primroses (*P. malacoides*) lines up below. Design: Sandra Jones.

Summer-long bouquet

Mixed planting of ferns with pink busy Lizzie (*Impatiens wallerana*) billows and trails so exuberantly that it conceals container from view. Kept in partial shade, airborne bouquet will bloom brightly all summer long.

Eye-level enchantment

Brimming over with brilliant bloom, purple and pink bougain-villea ('Crimson Jewel' and 'Rosenka', respectively) enchant the passerby from their suspended containers.

Summertime duet

Dangling from a tree limb, pink begonias harmonize with trailing blue lobelia in a spherical two-tone bouquet.

Fence flowers

Colorful camouflage for a tall redwood fence, mixed bouquets bloom from half-round wire baskets attached at varying heights. Assortment includes floss flower (*Ageratum*), begonias, marigolds (*Tagetes*), salvia, and zinnias—all requiring plenty of water and fertilizer to bloom profusely.

Trailing bouquet

Frothy cluster of yellow calceolaria, white impatiens, and pink ivy geranium (*Pelargonium peltatum*) splashes joyful colors against a dark wooden fence. Ground ivy (*Glechoma hederacea*) trails down. Design: Egon Molbak.

Living bouquets in moss-lined wire baskets

Suspended from tree limb or rafter, a living bouquet enchants everyone with its extravagance of flower color and greenery. A flower-filled basket is easy to make—you start with a moss-lined wire basket, then add plants to cover the bottom, sides, and top (see illustrations below). Flowering annuals are the most popular choices, but you can add variety with trailing ivy or lush green ferns. Set in plants all around a wire sphere to make a flower-covered ball; or, for a wall-hung floral bouquet, plant a half sphere.

You'll need an 820-cubic-inch bag of green sphagnum moss, potting soil mix (purchase a lightweight type or prepare your own batch of Extra Lightweight Mix—see page 95), and a wire basket. Most baskets are from 10 to 14 inches in diameter; the larger the basket, the heavier it will be after planting, especially just after watering. Baskets smaller than 10 inches in diameter will dry out quickly, requiring frequent watering.

Choose an assortment of cell-pack-size plants to cover the basket; favorite selections include marigolds, petunias, sweet alyssum, lobelia, and bedding begonias.

Space plants 2 to 6 inches apart, depending on the eventual size of the plant (check with the nursery salesperson). Use different plants to create attractive patterns of texture and color. If the young plants you buy already have a few blooms, your bouquet will look full in only 2 to 3 weeks.

Water the basket every other day, even daily in hot or windy weather; the moss should be slightly damp at all times. Fill to the top several times, or until water drips from the base. Or dunk the basket in a tub of water.

Colorful primrose (*Primula polyantha, P. malacoides*, and hybrid *P. juliae*), suspended high in midair, dazzle in all directions from their concealed wire basket. Airy, delicate blossoms of fairy primroses at top of basket contrast with more compact English and Juliana flowers.

Adequate amounts of fertilizer are essential to keep the basket bouquet alive and blooming. Every week, starting 2 weeks after planting, apply a complete liquid fertilizer at one-quarter the recommended monthly amount. Or add timed-release fertilizer to the soil mix before planting (reapply according to package directions).

Easy 4-step planting

1) Push soaking-wet moss through basket mesh from inside. Make moss lining 1 inch thick, extending 1 inch above rim.

2) Poke planting holes in moss with fingers or shears. Push roots through from outside while gently pulling from inside.

3) Fill lowest tier with flowers, then add enough lightweight potting soil mix to cover roots of plants completely. Tamp soil.

4) Continue planting in tiers as in step 3. Finally, plant to fill top opening of basket. Move to garden location; water gently.

Bouquets of living color

Planting a mixed bouquet brings out the artist in many a gardener. Blending colors, choosing just the right sizes and shapes—such design decisions offer as much pleasure as the showy results later on.

Annuals that bloom simultaneously are the most common choices for a mixed bouquet, but perennials and bulbs can also add striking beauty. Lacy ferns, ivy, and decorative herbs such as parsley are often added as accent plantings, enhancing the bouquet with extra touches of green. And just a scatter of white blossoms will intensify the hues of brightly colored flowers surrounding them.

As you design and plant a mixed bouquet, keep flower heights in mind. To achieve a full, rounded shape, aim for a gradation: place low, trailing plants at the container edge, medium-size ones just inside, and the tallest at the center.

For the most dramatic impact, use a container that's at least 18 inches wide. Space plants closely, about 4 inches apart; this will force them to grow upwards and out. In just a few weeks, they'll look like an abundant arrangement of cut flowers in a vase.

A container bouquet needs plenty of moisture; never let it dry out. Each week throughout the growing season, apply a complete fertilizer, diluted to one-quarter the recommended monthly amount. Remove faded blossoms regularly to encourage continued bloom.

In late May or June, many nurseries offer a wide selection of bedding annuals already in bloom. An easy way to plan a mixed bouquet is simply to work out its design right at the nursery, then take home the necessary plants and pot them together as envisioned.

Or you might prefer to follow this "recipe" (or use it as inspiration):

For a tall, multicolored bouquet, plant dark blue lobelia, red and white petunias, and orange and yellow nasturtiums (*Tropaeolum*) around the container edge. Midway to the center, plant yellow orange zinnias and yellow marigolds (*Tagetes*). At the center, set in pink, red, and white cosmos with tall gold marigolds and multihued painted-tongue (*Salpiglossis*).

Fountain of bloom

Like a fountain spilling with breathtaking bloom, snugly planted container mingles vivid red phlox with nemesia and dainty lobelia in varying shades of lavender. Design: Michael Westgard.

Misty splendor

Aglow with rich colors against the misty air, an array of container-grown bouquets display yellow and orange marigolds (*Tagetes*), white dwarf marguerites (*Chrysanthemum frutescens*), purple petunias, and red orange zinnias. Design: Kienholz/Kunkle, Inc.

The more, the merrier

One big, beautiful burst of color results from closely clustering three medium-size pots—hidden from view by the extravagance of the bouquet they support. Blossoms include cosmos, marigolds (*Tagetes*), nasturtiums (*Tropaeolum*), and flowering tobacco (*Nicotiana*).

Landscaping with containers   25

. . . Bouquets of living color

Geraniums & Co.

Potted pink geraniums (*Pelargonium*) accented with dainty violas and white sweet alyssum (*Lobularia maritima*) perch jauntily along lawns' edge.
Design: Lew Whitney of Rogers Gardens.

Dazzle of white

By vivid contrast, white marguerites (*Chrysanthemum frutescens*) seem to intensify the brilliance of red geraniums (*Pelargonium*).

Portable posies

Roll-around planter carts its floral cargo wherever you need instant color. Portable garden includes red and pink geraniums (*Pelargonium*), dwarf white marguerites (*Chrysanthemum frutescens*), blue and white petunias, dusty miller (*Senecio cineraria*), yellow marigolds (*Tagetes*), and lobelia.
Design: Michael Westgard.

Plants for shady places

Beneath a spreading tree, along a north-facing wall, under a patio overhead—you may find such shady spots the most inviting places in your garden. But many popular container plants simply refuse to thrive in shade. The temperature (noticeably lower than in sunny patches just a few feet away) is too cool for their liking, while the light intensity is too low to promote vigorous growth and bloom.

Fortunately, though, many other attractive plants either tolerate shade cheerfully or actually prefer it. Often native to forests or foggy regions, many of these plants long ago adapted to low-light conditions. You may even find that certain favorite plants grow better for you in shaded containers than they ever have in the open ground—all they needed was the special pampering of container life.

The cool, foliaged environment of a shady garden offers special satisfaction to people, too. On hot afternoons, it's just the spot for relaxing on a chaise with a good book and a tall, cool drink.

Here are some of the plants that might surround you as you take your ease—some blooming, others casting dappled shadows with their leaves. All are shade-lovers that perform splendidly in containers. (For full details, check the alphabetical listings under each category between pages 30 and 81.)

Cool, colorful oasis

In a quiet, shady garden corner, vivid red and pink begonias join white impatiens, ferns, and azaleas (not in bloom).

Annuals & perennials

Aspidistra elatior (Cast-iron plant)
Begonia
Browallia (Amethyst flower)
Campanula
Coleus hybridus (Coleus)
Digitalis (Foxglove)
Ferns
Hosta (Plantain lily)
Impatiens wallerana (Busy Lizzie)
Mimulus hybridus (Monkey flower)
Primula (Primrose)
Viola (Pansy and viola)

Shrubs

Aucuba japonica (Japanese aucuba)
Brunfelsia pauciflora (Yesterday-today-and-tomorrow)
Buxus (Boxwood)
Camellia

. . . Shrubs

Daphne odora (Winter daphne)
Fatsia japonica (Japanese aralia)
Fuchsia
Hydrangea
Ilex (Holly)
Nandina domestica (Heavenly bamboo)
Pieris japonica (Flame-of-the-forest)
Rhododendron (Rhododendrons and azaleas)

Trees

Ficus (Ornamental fig)
Laurus nobilis (Sweet bay)
Palms

Vines

Trachelospermum jasminoides (Star jasmine)
Tropaeolum (Nasturtium)

Seasonal performances

If the natural world were a stage, the drama played there would encompass four acts: spring, summer, autumn, and winter, each with spectacular changes of scenery and costume.

Many gardeners like to emphasize these changing scenes by displaying, in turn, some of the showiest plants of each season. Managing such stage direction is fairly easy with a container garden, because of its portability and relatively small scale. Here are a few ideas.

Starting as early as possible, plant spring bulbs chosen for a long sequence of bloom. Keep pots out of sight until they start to flower, then give them center stage. If you like, add a supporting cast of other spring show-stoppers—a flowering cherry (*Prunus*) or spring-blooming perennials. Meanwhile, backstage, start work on the next sequence of bloom—summer's annuals.

The annuals can continue from late spring until autumn's first frosts. As soft, leafy contrast to their brilliant colors, consider a tubbed Japanese maple (*Acer palmatum*) or European white birch (*Betula pendula*). As summer slips into autumn, either tree will open the next act with a blaze of burnished foliage. Add golden or orange chrysanthemums for a mellow autumnal mood.

Winter signals the poinsettias' entrance, along with red-berried holly (*Ilex*) or pyracantha. And any tubbed conifer brightens cold-weather gardens with welcome accents of green.

If you'd rather not rotate container plantings, you might prefer to display trees and shrubs that change their own "costumes"—often quite dramatically—with each season. Japanese maple, scarlet kadsura (*Kadsura japonica*), and heavenly bamboo (*Nandina domestica*) all perform such a role magnificently.

Summer's sunny colors

Sunny, summery flower color brightens deck edge. Showy effect results from grouping pots around 6-foot planter filled with red geraniums (*Pelargonium*) and Scotch pine. Container color comes from marguerites (*Chrysanthemum frutescens*), lobelia, lychnis, and marigolds (*Tagetes*). Design: R. David Adams Associates, Inc.

Springtime splendor

Magnificent heralds of the new growing season, 'Pink Supreme' and white 'Mt. Tacoma' tulips bloom in thickly clustered splendor from large tubs, surrounded by a chorus of purple violas and lobelia.

Winter's bright bouquets

Showy favorite of the holiday season, poinsettia (*Euphorbia pulcherrima*) thrives outdoors in mild-winter climates, otherwise offers cheerful indoor decoration. Its red or white "petals" are actually bracts (modified leaves). Surrounding three poinsettia bouquets in this garden corner are red and pink cyclamen, with rosemary in the background.

Autumn's eloquence

Japanese maple (*Acer palmatum*) offers a stunning seasonal show all on its own—leaves are red in spring, green through summer, then turn to burnished gold in autumn.

Favorite container plants

Whether you're looking for a brightly blooming annual or a twining vine, you'll find just the right container plant in this chapter. These are marguerites (*Chrysanthemum frutescens*), impatiens, begonias, bougainvillea, yew pine (*Podocarpus macrophyllus*), and *Lobelia* 'Sapphire'.

Virtually any plant can live in a container for a time—but for really reliable performers, choose from the plants described in this chapter. All were selected for their ability to adapt beautifully to life in contained quarters. These favorites accent their surroundings in dozens of ways, bringing color, drama, soothing shade, even edible fruit.

If you're not quite sure about the look you want, glance through the photographs on pages 4 to 29 for ideas. Then, study the sections of this chapter for help in deciding what specific plants are best for you.

The first two sections, annuals and perennials, offer a multitude of colorful choices for flower lovers. Try combining members of both groups—and while you're at it, bring in a few bulbs (from the next section) for their special magic of bloom and fragrance.

Vines, listed next, wander and billow wherever you want a leafy natural screen or a little greenery to soften a bare wall. They also look lovely cascading from a hanging basket.

If you need a touch of garden drama or some restful shade, consider potted shrubs and trees. Once established, most of these will give many years of graceful form, foliage, and seasonal color for a minimum of care.

Indoor-outdoor plants add leafy beauty inside when the weather is cold, then decorate deck or patio in the warm spring and summer months.

Our last sections list favorite plants for the gardening cook—or for anyone else who appreciates homegrown vegetables, herbs, fruits, and berries. You'll be delighted by the fresh-tasting abundance to be harvested from even a small collection of container-grown plants.

Annuals

Viola cornuta 'Imperial Orange' (viola) and *Lobularia maritima* (sweet alyssum)

If you're looking for brightly blossoming plants, annuals are for you. These adaptable plants perform admirably in pots, boxes, tubs, and hanging baskets. As the group's name indicates, annuals have a fairly short life span—a year or less—but they bloom constantly during much of this time.

All container-grown plants require attentive watering and fertilizing, but such care matters even more to annuals: they grow more rapidly, and bloom much more intensely, than longer-lived plants. You can grow annuals in almost any size container, as long as it's at least 6 inches deep—just be sure to space your plants 4 to 6 inches apart (plants are usually positioned closer together in containers than in the ground, for a fuller effect).

Pinch off tips to encourage bushy growth.

Before planting, gently untangle matted roots.

Growing from transplants

Most nurseries offer quite an assortment of annual transplants. You'll see small plants already in flower in the nursery's six-packs and flats; these are strains that have been bred to bloom while still young. You may want to buy them to add instant color to your garden. But as a rule, it's best to buy six-pack or flat-grown plants not yet in bloom; these perform better later on. Be picky: Look for healthy specimens that aren't extremely potbound or spindly looking. (If you really want to start with blooming plants, buy the larger annuals—in 4-inch or larger containers—sold at nurseries in late spring and early summer. These do well later on.)

Keep transplants shaded and well watered until you can plant them. Before planting, pinch off growing tips (see drawing above) of any types that tend to get leggy—cosmos, marigold (*Tagetes*), and zinnia, for example. If flower buds are present, pinch those off too.

Remove plants from their nursery pots as described on page 96. Open up matted roots at the bottom of the soil ball (see drawing at left), or gently pull circled roots away from the sides. Proceed with planting as described on pages 96 to 97. In areas with hot, sunny spring and summer weather, plant in the cool of the evening. Until plants are well established (about 2 weeks), keep in a place that's shady during the hottest afternoon hours. Keep soil moist during this period, but don't fertilize until plants are actively growing.

Growing from seed

If you have time, you can save money by starting annuals from seed. Both nurseries and garden catalogs offer a wide selection. For best results, use seeds packed for the current year (check the date stamped on the seed packet).

To plant, simply sow seeds into containers filled with a moistened lightweight potting soil mix, following packet directions. Cover seeds with a thin layer of equal parts sand and soil mix; keep pots shaded and soil moist until seeds have sprouted above the soil surface. When seedlings are a few inches tall, move pots to provide plants with the amount of light they need and thin seedlings to 4 to 6 inches apart. Start fertilizing 4 weeks or so later.

Ageratum
Floss flower

Pictured on pages 10, 22

Floss flower typically has blossoms of powder blue, but you'll also find hybrid forms with white or pinkish white blooms. Size ranges from 6 inches to 2 feet; most types are between 9 and 18 inches tall.

When selecting this annual for container growing, look for relatively small and compact types in the color you prefer. In full flower, these will give the most pleasing shape, with a look of overall softness.

Plant floss flower seeds or transplants in spring, spacing plants 4 to 6 inches apart (thin seedlings accordingly). Use a lightweight potting soil mix, and keep it moist—if soil is allowed to dry out repeatedly, plants will never really completely recover. In hot, dry climates, give morning sun only or filtered sun all day. Elsewhere, a full-sun location is best. Apply a complete fertilizer monthly (apply timed-release fertilizer less often, following package directions).

Floss flower blooms from late spring through summer. To keep plants tidy and prolong the blooming period, trim off faded flowers.

Antirrhinum majus
Snapdragon

Pictured on page 10

An old-fashioned favorite that many remember fondly from childhood, snapdragons have acquired a new look in recent years. Standard "snapping" blooms are still widely available—but in some strains, the "snapping" flower has disappeared. In its place, you'll find double blossoms like small hollyhocks, bell-shaped flowers, or even azalealike double-bell-shaped blooms. In all types, blossoms cling to upright flower spikes; buds at the stalk base are the first to bloom.

You can grow snapdragon in three sizes: dwarf (to 8 inches), intermediate (12 to 20 inches), and tall (2 to 3 feet). Unless you don't mind staking the plants, choose dwarf or intermediate sizes for containers.

Where winters are frost free, plant snapdragon seeds or transplants in a sunny spot in early autumn; they'll bloom in winter and early spring. In cold-winter areas, plant in early spring for late spring and summer bloom. Space plants 4 to 6 inches apart (thin seedlings accordingly).

Plant seeds or transplants in a lightweight potting soil mix; keep soil moist, but not soggy. From spring through summer, apply a complete fertilizer monthly (apply timed-release fertilizer less often, following package directions).

Snapdragon's worst enemy is the disease called rust—so always buy a rust-resistant strain (these are widely available in both seeds and transplants). If rust develops, use one of the controls listed on page 108, and be sure to avoid wetting foliage.

Begonia semperflorens-cultorum
Bedding begonia, wax begonia

Pictured on pages 13, 16, 22, 27, 30

Bedding begonias have long been a favorite choice for flowerpots that sit in shade or semishade. It's easy to understand their popularity: they're easy to care for, and they produce an abundance of blossoms over a long blooming season. Depending on the type, bedding begonias grow from 6 to 18 inches high in a compact and bushy form. Glossy leaves may be green, bronzy green, or bronzy red. Flowers—single or double—come in white and shades of pink and red. Blossoms are typically about an inch wide, but in some strains they're as big as 3 inches across.

Bedding begonias are actually tender perennials—where winters are frost free, they'll bloom almost all year round. Elsewhere, expect summer-through-autumn bloom.

Bedding begonia seeds are difficult to start, so it's easiest to begin with transplants. Set out plants in spring, spacing them 4 to 6 inches apart. Use a lightweight potting soil mix, and keep it moist, but not soggy. Apply a complete fertilizer once a month from spring through summer (apply timed-release fertilizer less often, following package directions). Bedding begonias like a partial-shade location.

Browallia
Amethyst flower, browallia

Pictured below and on page 34

This attractive, shade-loving plant deserves greater popularity. Two species are commonly available; both bloom outdoors all summer long, offering white, violet, or blue flowers with white throats.

Browallia americana's branching stems grow 1 to 2 feet tall, carrying many clusters of ½-inch flowers. *B. speciosa* sprawls when mature, draping attractively from a hanging container. Standard types of this species grow 2 to 3 feet tall;

dwarf forms become quite bushy and stand just 12 to 15 inches tall.

In spring, plant amethyst flower seeds or transplants in a mix of two-thirds lightweight potting soil mix, one-third peat moss. Space plants 4 to 6 inches apart (thin seedlings accordingly). Keep soil moist, but not soggy. Every 2 weeks, apply a complete fertilizer at half the recommended monthly amount. (Apply timed-release fertilizer less often, following package directions.) Place containers in partial shade.

When weather cools in autumn, bring amethyst flower indoors, cut back halfway, and place in a cool window receiving bright reflected light. After a few months of rest, plants will continue to bloom all winter.

Calendula officinalis
Calendula, pot marigold

During the cool months of the year, calendula produces masses of long-lasting flowers in warm, sunny colors. Where winters are frost free, it blooms all winter long; in cold-winter areas, it's one of the first

Browallia speciosa 'Blue Bells' (amethyst flower)

flowers to herald spring. The bushy plants grow from 1 to 3 feet tall, producing single, double, or semidouble blossoms in profusion. (Dwarf forms are also available.) You'll find the 2½ to 4½-inch flowers in cream, yellow, gold, and various shades of orange.

Calendula is easy to grow from seed. Plant in autumn (where winters are frost free) or early spring; thin seedlings to 4 to 6 inches apart (or set out nursery transplants accordingly). Use a lightweight potting soil mix, and keep it moist, but not soggy. From spring through summer, apply a complete fertilizer once a month (apply timed-release fertilizer less often, following package directions). For the most abundant blooms, place in full sun.

Callistephus chinensis
China aster

Question: What looks like a riotously colorful, oversize outdoor bouquet? Answer: A container full of China asters. These big, showy flowers of red, pink, white, purple, and lavender blue have delighted gardeners for generations. Dwarf types, growing about 1 foot tall, do best in containers. Taller forms (to 3 feet) are also available, but these look a bit ungainly when planted in pots.

All sorts of different flower forms are available: petals may be quilled, curled, incurved, ribbonlike, or in interlaced rays. Some blooms have crested centers. You'll also see varieties labeled as "pompon," "peony-flowered," "anemone-flowered," and "ostrich feather"; these names give a fair description of flower shape.

Plant seeds or transplants in spring, spacing plants 4 to 6 inches apart (thin seedlings accordingly). Use a lightweight potting soil mix. Keep soil moist, but not soggy; apply a complete fertilizer once a month (apply timed-release fertilizer less often, following package directions). Place pots in full sun.

Catharanthus roseus
Madagascar periwinkle

Lasting long after zinnias and marigolds have faded, Madagascar periwinkle blooms from spring right up until Thanksgiving if weather stays mild. The five-petaled, 1½-inch-wide flowers nestle among glossy green leaves; you'll find them in blush pink, bright pink, pure white, and white marked with a red or rose colored "eye."

This bushy 1 to 2-foot plant is a good choice for hot-summer areas, thriving even in desert gardens. Though technically a perennial, it's usually grown as an annual.

You can start Madagascar periwinkle from seeds or transplants; nurseries sometimes sell it as *Vinca rosea* (its former name). Plant in spring, in a mix of half garden loam, half lightweight potting soil mix. Space plants 6 inches apart (thin seedlings accordingly). Let soil dry out almost completely between waterings.

During the blooming season, apply a complete fertilizer monthly (apply timed-release fertilizer less often, following package directions). Give full sun or partial shade.

Centaurea cyanus
Bachelor's button, cornflower

Pictured on page 9

This old-fashioned favorite blooms all summer long, bearing 1½-inch blossoms amid finely cut gray green foliage. The most familiar flower color is bright blue, but modern forms of bachelor's button also offer blossoms in pink, wine, red, and white (some bicolors are available, as well). Standard types reach a height of 2 to 3 feet; dwarf forms are only 1 foot tall.

It's easy to grow bachelor's button from seed. Plant in spring, in containers filled with a lightweight pot-

ting soil mix; thin seedlings to 4 to 6 inches apart (or set out nursery transplants accordingly). Allow soil to dry out somewhat between waterings. Apply a complete fertilizer once a month (apply timed-release fertilizer less often, following package directions). Bachelor's button does best in full sun.

Cosmos
Cosmos

Pictured on pages 8, 24

This wide-branched, willowy plant comes in two commonly available forms, both producing a multitude of daisylike flowers in summer. The common cosmos, *Cosmos bipinnatus,* has single blossoms in white and shades of lavender, magenta, and pink, all with tufted yellow centers. It grows from 2 to 6 feet tall. *C. sulphureus,* the second species, may grow to 7 feet—but for containers, choose one of the new, more compact hybrid forms. These little plants reach just 2 to 3 feet. *C. sulphureus* has double or semidouble flowers in colors of gold, orange, and vermilion (some have striped petals).

Because these two species of cosmos have different color ranges, they're not particularly attractive when planted together. Both types are a bit rangy; to conceal their lankiness, set shorter, bushier companion plants around their bases.

Cosmos is easily grown from seed. Plant in spring; thin seedlings to 4 to 6 inches apart (or set out nursery transplants accordingly). Use a lightweight potting soil mix. Keep soil moist, but not soggy; apply a complete fertilizer once a month (apply timed-release fertilizer less often, following package directions). Cosmos likes full sun. To prolong the blooming season, regularly remove spent flowers.

Dianthus barbatus (sweet William)

Dianthus barbatus
Sweet William

Pictured on page 33

This relative of the carnation has enhanced flower gardens for hundreds of years. It has carnationlike gray green foliage; the finely marked flowers, carnationlike in shape, bloom in clusters of white, rich red, pink, or purple (you'll find some bicolor, as well). These 10 to 20-inch-tall plants look best grouped close together or as part of a container bouquet. They combine well with other old-fashioned favorites, such as stock (*Matthiola*), nemesia, and foxglove (*Digitalis*).

For midspring bloom, set out transplants in early spring, spacing them 4 to 6 inches apart. (Started from seed, most types won't bloom until the year after planting.) Use a lightweight potting soil mix, and keep it moist, but not soggy. Apply a complete fertilizer once a month (apply timed-release fertilizer less often, following package directions).

Sweet William tolerates frosts, but it can't take extreme heat. Give full sun only where summers are mild; elsewhere, filtered sun is best.

Impatiens wallerana (busy Lizzie, impatiens) and *Browallia*

Helianthus
Sunflower

Those familiar sunflowers that produce seeds for snacking grow far too tall for most plant containers. But you can find new sunflower types that take very nicely to large containers (see page 84).

'Dwarf Sungold' and 'Teddy Bear' are both multibranched plants that grow only 1½ to 2 feet high, producing a sunny profusion of 4-inch double flowers with dark centers. Though unsurpassed for their cheery brilliance, these dwarf sunflowers rarely produce edible seeds.

Sunflowers are easily grown from seed. Plant in spring; thin seedlings to 4 to 6 inches apart (or set out nursery transplants accordingly). Use a lightweight potting soil mix; let soil dry out slightly between waterings. Apply a complete fertilizer once a month (apply timed-release fertilizer less often, following package directions). Given full sun, sunflowers will bloom from midsummer to the first frosts of autumn.

Iberis
Candytuft

Valued for its clusters of bright white flowers, annual candytuft blooms from spring through summer. *Iberis amara* (hyacinth-flowered candytuft) reaches a height of 1½ feet; it produces fragrant white blossoms on short spikes. *I. umbellata,* the globe candytuft, forms bushy, spreading plants up to a foot tall, ideal for container bouquet plantings. Globe candytuft is also available in a dwarf form; this type grows only 6 inches tall.

Plant seeds or transplants in spring, spacing plants 4 to 6 inches apart (thin seedlings accordingly). Use a lightweight potting soil mix, and keep it moist, but not soggy.

Apply a complete fertilizer once a month (apply timed-release fertilizer less often, following package directions). Candytuft likes full sun except in hot-summer areas, where it prefers filtered sun or partial shade.

To keep plants compact and prolong the blooming season, regularly trim off spent flowers.

Impatiens
Balsam, busy Lizzie, impatiens

Pictured below left and on pages 5, 6, 19, 21, 22, 27, 30, 63

You'll find three basic groups of impatiens at your nursery: *Impatiens balsamina* (balsam), *I. wallerana* (busy Lizzie, impatiens), and the New Guinea hybrids. All bloom as profusely in pots as they do in the open ground; in fact, the New Guinea hybrids do better in containers.

Balsam (*I. balsamina*) has been perking up gardens with its summer-through-autumn blooms since Grandma's day. Growing from 10 to 30 inches tall, it has 2 to 6-inch leaves and flowers in white or shades of pink or lilac. In some varieties, blossoms are double.

A second, more modern group of impatiens (*I. wallerana*) goes by the common name of busy Lizzie. Available types range from 4 to 8-inch dwarfs on up to 2-foot standard-size varieties. There's a wide range of flower colors—you'll see blooms in red, pink, rose, violet, orange, and white, along with some bicolors. Flowers are mostly single, though there are some double types. The pale green, succulent stems bear glossy dark green leaves.

Unsurpassed for bringing color to shady areas, busy Lizzie blooms from spring to the first autumn frosts with a minimum of gardener's effort. For a spectacular splash of color, grow it in a hanging basket. If plants don't dangle sufficiently at first, let them wilt slightly, then resume watering.

They'll regain their vigor, but keep the drooping posture. (Note: Don't try this watering technique with other annuals.)

Plant balsam and busy Lizzie transplants in spring, in a lightweight potting soil mix. Space plants 4 to 6 inches apart. Give them plenty to drink—both types need more water than most plants. What they don't need to excess is fertilizer: overfed, they produce thick, luxuriant foliage at the expense of flowers. Apply a complete fertilizer only every 6 weeks or so. Place containers in a location receiving either full shade or morning sun only.

Newest on the impatiens scene are members of the third group, the New Guinea hybrids. These recent arrivals from New Guinea offer blooms in red, pink, orange, lavender, and purple. Their wildly colorful leaves, often variegated with yellow or red, may look brighter than the flowers. Plants grow from 1½ to 2 feet tall.

Plant New Guinea hybrid impatiens in spring for summer-through-autumn bloom. Set out transplants in containers filled with a lightweight potting soil mix, spacing them 4 to 6 inches apart. Keep soil moist, but not soggy. Every 2 weeks, apply a complete fertilizer mixed at half the recommended monthly amount. (Apply timed-release fertilizer less often, following package directions). These hybrids need more light than other types of impatiens to promote attractive flowering; place them in a spot where they'll receive filtered sun.

Lathyrus odoratus
Sweet pea

Pictured on page 7

Almost everyone knows and loves the splendid sight and smell of sweet peas, but few consider planting these summer-blooming beauties in a pot. Available today are several bushy, self-supporting varieties that look glorious when massed in a large container (see page 84). Offering the same color range as the usual vining sweet peas, bush varieties bloom in white and every pastel shade but yellow. 'Bijou', 'Jet Set', 'Knee-Hi', and 'Little Sweethearts' grow from 12 to 30 inches tall.

In spring (or autumn, where winters are frost free), plant seeds or transplants 4 to 6 inches apart in containers filled with a special soil mix of two parts garden loam, one part peat moss, ground bark, or sawdust. Before planting seeds, moisten soil mix well; then apply a complete fertilizer, following package directions. For faster germination, soak seeds for several hours before planting. Then, to give plants a safer start in life, shake seeds in a bag with powdered fungicide. Place containers in full sunlight. After seeds sprout, screen container to protect young seedlings from birds (see page 108). You'll also need to put out bait for slugs and snails (see page 109).

Sweet peas appreciate moist soil and a bimonthly dose of a complete fertilizer at half the recommended monthly amount. (Timed-release fertilizer can be applied less often; follow package directions.)

Lobelia erinus
Lobelia

Pictured on pages 1, 5, 6, 8, 9, 15, 17, 19, 22, 24, 26, 28, 30

Lobelia blooms all summer long, in pure white, pale lavender to deep purple, and intense shades of sky blue to sapphire. Its small, tubular, three-lipped flowers cover compact (clumping) or trailing plants. Trailing lobelia makes a lovely border for a container bouquet (see page 24), draping gracefully over the pot rim.

In spring, plant lobelia seeds or transplants in a lightweight potting soil mix, spacing plants 4 to 6 inches apart (thin seedlings accordingly). Keep soil moist, but not soggy. Apply a complete fertilizer once a month. (Apply timed-release fertilizer less often, following package directions). Place in full sun where summers are cool; where weather is hot and dry, give plants partial shade.

Lobularia maritima
Sweet alyssum

Pictured on pages 9, 10, 15, 26, 31

This low-growing, trailing plant is especially lovely in combination with other flowers. When in bloom, it forms a solid mound of small, fragrant blossoms—white, purple, or rosy pink.

It's easy to grow sweet alyssum from seed. Plant in early spring, in containers filled with a lightweight potting soil mix; thin seedlings to 4 to 6 inches apart (or set out nursery transplants accordingly). Let soil dry out somewhat between waterings. Every 6 weeks or so, apply a complete fertilizer. Plants do best in bright sun.

After initial flowering in late spring or summer, cut sweet alyssum back halfway; this promotes a second wave of bloom and keeps plants from becoming rangy.

Matthiola incana
Stock

Pictured at right and on page 15

Beloved for its spicy fragrance, stock produces spikes of single or double blossoms in late spring and summer. The wide range of flower color includes purple, magenta, lavender, rose, pink, cream, and white. Dwarf varieties, reaching a height of 1 to 1½ feet, are best for containers; taller types of stock (to 3 feet) usually need staking.

Where winters are frost free, plant seeds or transplants in autumn; elsewhere, plant in early spring. Space plants 4 to 6 inches apart (thin seedlings accordingly). Use a lightweight potting soil mix; keep soil moist, but not soggy. From spring through summer, apply a complete fertilizer once a month (apply timed-release fertilizer less often, following package directions). Stock prefers full sun, but will also tolerate partial shade.

Mimulus hybridus
Mimulus, monkey flower

New hybrids of mimulus, more vigorous and attractive than the older types, will probably increase the popularity of this little-known annual. Hybrid forms grow 1 to 2 feet tall; in summer, they bear a profusion of 2½-inch flowers in shades of brilliant gold, red, or yellow, sometimes strikingly mottled with brown or maroon.

Plant mimulus seeds or transplants in spring, spacing plants 4 to 6 inches apart (thin seedlings accordingly). Use a lightweight potting soil mix enriched with peat moss (one-third to one-half the total container volume). Keep soil moist—never let it dry out completely between waterings. Every 2 weeks, apply a complete fertilizer at half the recommended monthly amount. (Apply timed-release fertilizer less often, following package directions.) Mimulus doesn't like direct sun or deep shade; it needs a cool spot receiving filtered sun or partial shade. (Without just the right light conditions, it may refuse to grow.)

Bring mimulus indoors before the first autumn frost, cut back halfway, and place in a window receiving bright reflected light. After a brief rest period, it will bloom all winter long.

Nemesia strumosa
Nemesia

Pictured on pages 15, 24

A cool-season annual, nemesia blazes with every possible flower color except green—you'll find blossoms in clear yellow, vivid orange, rich pink, deep ruby red, and more. A small white-and-purple detail on the throat makes each flower look even brighter. Several plants massed together make a brilliant display. Plants grow from 10 to 18 inches high, though a lower, more compact form ('Nana Compacta') is also available. Nemesia looks particularly striking when planted with bright blue lobelia (see entry at left) in a hanging container.

In spring (or in autumn, where winters are frost free) plant seeds or transplants in a lightweight potting soil mix, spacing plants 4 to 6 inches apart (thin seedlings accordingly). Keep soil moist, but not soggy. To coax bushiness, pinch growing tips of standard-size plants when they reach a height of 2 to 3 inches. Apply a complete fertilizer at half the recommended monthly amount every 2 weeks. (If you use timed-release fertilizer, you won't need to apply it as often; follow package directions.) Kept in the sun, nemesia blooms heavily from late spring until it fades with the summer heat.

Matthiola incana (stock)

Nicotiana
Flowering tobacco

Pictured on page 24

In old-fashioned fragrance gardens, flowering tobacco filled the air with a sweet, heady perfume—but only in the evening or on cloudy days. Now you can find modern hybrids that open their fragrant summertime blooms all day long, in any weather. Trumpet-shaped flowers in a variety of colors—lime, mauve, maroon, pink, red, and white—top 1 to 3-foot stems; large, fuzzy leaves encircle stem bases. Flowering tobacco looks attractive when surrounded by lower-growing, draping plants.

Plant flowering tobacco seeds or transplants in spring, spacing plants about 6 inches apart (thin seedlings accordingly). Use a lightweight potting soil mix, and keep it moist, but not soggy. Apply a complete fertilizer once a month (apply timed-release fertilizer less often, following package directions). In hot-summer areas, place in partial shade; elsewhere, give full sun.

This plant is actually a tender perennial; in mild-winter climates, it may live from one year to the next.

Petunia hybrida (petunia)

Petunia hybrida
Petunia

Pictured below and on pages 8, 9, 18, 25, 26

Among the most popular of annuals, petunias offer lavish summertime color that can't fail to please. Their ruffly, trumpet-shaped single or double blossoms range in color from soft pink to deepest red, pale blue to richest purple, along with white and assorted shades of cream and yellow.

Petunias are generally classed as either Grandiflora or Multiflora. Blossoms of Grandiflora petunias are large—up to 4½ inches across. Multifloras produce many more blooms than Grandifloras, but flowers are also smaller—only about 2 inches across. One popular Grandiflora for hanging pots and tall containers is 'Cascade': the plants drape and trail beautifully. The Satin series of Multifloras, with neat, compact growth, are ideal for massing in a tub or planter.

If you want a petunia to show off at close range, try one of the 'Giants of California'—an unusual group that's neither Grandiflora nor Multiflora. Big, frilly, 4 to 6-inch flowers flaunt showy markings at the throat.

Plant all types of petunias in spring. Set out transplants in a lightweight potting soil mix, spacing plants 4 to 6 inches apart (thin seedlings accordingly). Keep soil moist, but not soggy. Apply a complete fertilizer once a month (apply timed-release fertilizer less often, following package directions). In smoggy areas, seedlings' leaves may show spots; as smog clears, plants will produce new, unspotted leaves.

Give petunias full sun all day except in hot-summer areas—here, place in a location receiving morning sun only. When plants reach a height of 3 to 4 inches, trim them back halfway to encourage bushiness. As summer draws to a close, cut rangy plants back about halfway and apply a dose of fertilizer to stimulate a second bloom (2 to 3 weeks after cutting back).

Phlox drummondii
Annual phlox

Pictured on page 24

Showy and abundant from summer through autumn, phlox blossoms cluster atop 6 to 18-inch-tall stems. Various strains offer bright and pastel shades of every hue but blue and orange; some flowers are centered with a contrasting "eye." Six-inch-tall dwarf strains, especially nice in containers, include Beauty (smooth-edged flowers) and Twinkle (fringed, starry flowers). All types of phlox are attractive planted with low-growing white or blue-flowered plants.

In spring, plant annual phlox seeds or transplants in a lightweight potting soil mix, spacing plants 4 to 6 inches apart—thin seedlings accordingly. (In mild climates, you can plant in autumn.) Keep soil moist, but not soggy; to avoid mildew, try not to wet foliage when watering. Apply a complete fertilizer once a month (apply timed-release fertilizer less often, following package directions). Phlox needs lots of sunshine for the most abundant bloom, so place pots in full sun.

Portulaca grandiflora
Portulaca, moss rose

Portulaca grandiflora's foliage resembles a thick, low-growing, coarse moss; its summer-blooming flowers, colored vivid lavender, magenta, orange, red, white, or yellow, look like single or double roses. These characteristics have given the plant one of its common names, "moss rose." In fact, though, it's neither rose nor moss (nor is it a true succulent, despite its succulent-looking foliage).

Portulaca grows up to 6 inches tall, with creeping stems that can wander 1½ feet or farther. These gracefully trailing plants are attractive in terra cotta bowls or near the edge of a large mixed planting.

In spring, plant portulaca seeds or transplants in a lightweight potting soil mix, spacing plants 4 to 6 inches apart (thin seedlings accordingly). Allow soil to dry out somewhat between waterings. Every 4 to 6 weeks, apply a complete fertilizer (apply timed-release fertilizer less often, following package directions). Portulaca needs full sun to thrive and blossom.

Salpiglossis sinuata
Painted-tongue

This exotic relative of the petunia grows in an upright, wide-branched shape, reaching a height of 2 to 3 feet. Painted-tongue blossoms are shaped like petunias, but their coloring is more varied: shades of mahogany, red, reddish orange, yellow, purple, and pink, all marbled and intricately etched with contrasting tones.

Plant seeds or transplants in spring; for a massed effect, space plants 3 to 4 inches apart (thin seedlings accordingly). Use a lightweight potting soil mix. When plants are young, give them plenty of water: keep soil moist (but not soggy) at all times. Give less water as plants mature, allowing soil to dry out somewhat between waterings. Apply a complete fertilizer once a month (apply timed-release fertilizer less often, following package directions). Give painted-tongue a full-sun or partial-shade location that's well protected from wind.

Salvia splendens
Salvia, scarlet sage

Pictured on page 22

Eye-catching spires of dazzling scarlet flowers explain this popular annual's appeal. Try grouping it with white or blue-flowered plants, or those with gray green foliage.

You can buy either standard-size or dwarf forms of salvia. Dwarf types generally grow 8 to 16 inches tall; standards may reach 30 inches. Though red is the most common color, salvia is also available in pink, deep purple, and white.

In spring, plant seeds or transplants in a lightweight potting soil mix, spacing plants 4 to 6 inches apart (thin seedlings accordingly). Keep soil moist, but not soggy. Apply a complete fertilizer once a month. (Apply timed-release fertilizer less

often, following package directions.) For best bloom—from late spring through the first autumn frosts— give salvia a full-sun location.

Schizanthus pinnatus
Butterfly flower

Pictured on pages 6, 7

Pink, rose, lilac, purple, or white clouds of tiny, yellow-throated orchidlike flowers reward the gardener who grows butterfly flower. Fernyfoliaged and reaching a height of about 1½ feet, it looks like a delicate bouquet when in bloom. Butterfly flower combines well with other cool-season favorites such as cineraria (*Senecio hybridus,* at right) and fairy primrose (*Primula malacoides,* page 44). Where winters are frost free, it blooms in late winter and early spring; elsewhere, look for summertime bloom.

Plant seeds or transplants in spring (or in autumn, where winters are frost free), in a lightweight potting soil mix. Space plants 4 to 6 inches apart (thin seedlings accordingly). Keep soil moist, but not soggy. From spring through summer, apply a complete fertilizer monthly. (If you use timed-release fertilizer, you can apply it less often; follow package directions.) For best blossoms, give butterfly flower filtered sun.

Senecio hybridus
Cineraria

Pictured below left

Borne atop 12 to 15-inch stems, cineraria's clusters of daisylike flowers bloom in clear, pure colors— blue, shining white, magenta, pink, and purple. In some types, flowers are ringed with concentric bands of white. Cinerarias are at their peak in cool weather. Where winters are frost free, they bloom in late winter and early spring; in cold-winter areas, expect flowers from spring until early summer.

Cinerarias are difficult to grow from seed, so it's best to start with nursery transplants. Plant in spring (in autumn where winters are frost free), spacing plants 4 to 6 inches apart. Use a lightweight potting soil mix; keep it moist at all times, but don't let it get soggy. Every 2 weeks from spring through summer, apply a complete fertilizer at half the recommended amount. (Apply timed-release fertilizer less often, following package directions.) Give cinerarias a cool location with partial shade or filtered sun.

Tagetes
Marigold

Pictured on pages 4, 6, 8, 9, 22, 24, 25, 26, 28

Marigolds' dizzying variety of size and color can create a dilemma for indecisive gardeners. Plants may be anywhere from 6 inches to 3 or more feet tall, and the range of blossom size is just as great—from ¾-inch petites to 5-inch giants, either single or double. Colors include solid or mixed shades of maroon, dark red, orange, yellow, cream, and white.

Though the wide, wonderful choice might lead you to believe otherwise, there are really only three commonly planted marigold types. African marigolds (*Tagetes erecta*) come in standard-size types (2½ to 3 feet) and in many dwarf forms (14 to

20 inches). French marigolds (*T. patula*) offer many mixed colors and range from 6 to 18 inches tall. The unusual signet marigold (*T. tenuifolia*) is a semitrailing form growing to 8 inches tall. It has finely cut, ferny foliage and an abundance of small flowers. All types of marigolds bloom from summer through autumn.

In spring, plant seeds or transplants of these widely available annuals in a lightweight potting soil mix. Space plants 4 to 6 inches apart (thin seedlings accordingly). Keep soil moist—never let it dry out between waterings. (Try to avoid wetting the flowers and foliage.) Apply a complete fertilizer once a month (apply timed-release fertilizer less often, following package directions). For best bloom, place containers in full sun.

Torenia fournieri
Torenia, wishbone flower

This compact, bushy plant stands just 1 foot tall. It blooms from late spring through summer, producing a multitude of tiny yellow-throated flowers that look like miniature gloxinias. Blossoms are typically light blue marked with deeper blue, but a white form is also available. Because of its diminutive size and the intricate coloration of its flowers, torenia is best appreciated from close up. Attractive partners for this plant include bedding begonias (page 32) and trailing lobelia (page 35)—or try combining it with pots of delicate green ferns.

In spring, plant torenia seeds or transplants in a lightweight potting soil mix, spacing plants 4 to 6 inches apart (thin seedlings accordingly). Keep soil moist, but not soggy; apply a complete fertilizer once a month (apply timed-release fertilizer less often, following package directions). In general, torenia prefers partial shade, but it can take full sun in mildsummer areas.

Senecio hybridus (cineraria)

Tropaeolum majus
Nasturtium

Pictured on page 24

This familiar, easy-to-grow favorite is available in bush type as well as in semitrailing and vining forms (see page 53). Bush-type nasturtiums grow in a mounded shape, reaching a height of 8 to 15 inches. All kinds of *T. majus* have round leaves and abundant single or double blossoms in every imaginable warm color—from root-beer brown, through red, pink, and orange, to yellow and cream. The blooming season lasts from spring right through autumn.

Nasturtiums don't transplant well, so you'll need to sow their large seeds directly into a container. Plant seeds as soon as weather warms in spring, following seed packet directions. Use a lightweight potting soil mix, and keep soil moist, but not soggy. Give plants no fertilizer at all; excessive nutrients slow flower formation. Nasturtiums grow well in either sun or shade, but bloom most abundantly in a brightly sunny spot (or in filtered sun, where summers are very hot). In mild-winter areas, these plants will live more than one season—they're actually tender perennials.

Verbena
Verbena

Pictured below and on pages 6, 8, 16

Verbena is technically a perennial, but it's most often grown as an annual. Its flat floral clusters glow with bright color atop low, spreading stems. Garden verbena (*Verbena hybrida*) grows 6 to 12 inches high, spreading 1½ to 3 feet or more. Its summertime blooms, sometimes scented, are available in red, pink, white, blue, purple, and combinations of these colors. Peruvian verbena (*V. peruviana*) spreads quickly, forming a low mat studded with red, white, pink, or purple flowers.

Both types are sun-loving, heat-tolerant plants; either makes a good-looking, quickly established "ground cover" in a planter. When planted near the edge of a container, verbena trails gracefully over the rim.

In spring, plant transplants in a lightweight potting soil mix, spacing plants 4 to 6 inches apart. Allow soil to dry out somewhat between waterings. Apply a complete fertilizer once a month (apply timed-release fertilizer less often, following package directions). Verbena thrives in the hottest, sunniest locations.

Viola
Pansies, violas

Pictured on pages 1, 7, 10, 11, 19, 26, 28, 31, 78

These cheery, compact little plants (usually under 8 inches tall) brighten the shady corners of the garden from early spring until summer's heat arrives. Pansies (*Viola wittrockiana*) produce flowers 2 to 4 inches wide in blue, purple, yellow, apricot, orange, mahogany red, white, and bicolors. Stripes or dark blotches usually decorate the petals. Multiflora types have smaller, more numerous flowers. Violas (*V. cornuta*) produce 1½-inch flowers, mostly in solid colors of yellow, apricot, ruby red, blue, purple, and white.

In early spring, (or in autumn, where winters are frost free), plant pansy and viola transplants in a lightweight potting soil mix, spacing plants 4 to 6 inches apart. Keep soil moist, but not soggy. Every 4 to 6 weeks, apply a complete fertilizer (apply timed-release fertilizer less often, following package directions). Place containers in a cool location receiving partial shade or filtered sun; remove faded flowers regularly to assure continuous bloom.

Zinnia
Zinnia

Pictured below and on pages 22, 25

This hot-weather favorite offers a great variety of flower shape and size—neat-as-a-pin or shaggy, 1-inch "buttons" or 7-inch giants. Your choice of flower color is just as wide: you'll find blooms in bright white and in dazzling shades of red, orange, pink, and yellow. (In fact, blue is the only hue missing from the zinnia palette.) Plant height ranges from 6 inches to 3 feet. Obviously, shorter varieties are best for most containers.

In spring, plant zinnia seeds or transplants in a lightweight potting soil mix, spacing plants 4 to 6 inches apart (thin seedlings accordingly). Give enough water to keep growth steady, but don't overwater. Apply a complete fertilizer monthly (apply timed-release fertilizer less often, following package directions). Zinnias thrive in the hottest, sunniest locations.

Powdery mildew (page 108) is a common problem for these plants. To prevent it, be careful not to wet leaves when you water—pour water on soil only.

Verbena hybrida (verbena)

Zinnia elegans (zinnia)

Container rock gardens

Though no one else fusses over them quite as devotedly as the English do, rock gardens are also dear to many Americans. If you haven't the time or space for a full-size rockery, you can easily establish one of these charming gardens in a container.

A typical rock garden looks like a mountain landscape in miniature, with clusters of plants tucked between rocks of various sizes. The plants favored for this rocky scene include quite a variety of forms and colors, but they do have several common characteristics. All are quite small, ranging in size from ground-hugging creepers only a few inches tall to shrubbier specimens reaching about 2 feet. Flowers and leaves are correspondingly diminutive, sometimes scarcely bigger than teardrops. And as you'd expect, these plants prefer rather coarse, gritty soil.

True rock-garden devotees like to choose their plants from a subgroup called Alpines: natives of high-altitude regions in Switzerland, Austria, and other mountainous regions throughout the world. But other plants, too, are lovely in rockeries (Alpines can be difficult to grow at lower elevations).

Pots protect plants

Removed from their natural environment, rock garden plants often take more successfully to containers than to life in the open ground. A container home protects them from the hazards to which small plants are particularly vulnerable—and displays them to best advantage. And when you set up your rockery in a pot, it's especially easy to supply plants with the gritty soil they need to thrive.

Choose a wide, shallow container—only about 6 to 8 inches deep. One traditional choice is a stone trough; concrete cast in a trough shape makes an attractive modern substitute. Fill the container with a mix of equal parts coarse peat moss, leaf mold, fine gravel, and river or quarry sand. (Don't use beach sand.) Arrange a few carefully chosen rocks on the soil surface; then set in plants, tucking them around rocks. Finally, apply a thin gravel mulch to help keep soil cool and to protect low-lying foliage from contact with moist soil (moisture can rot leaves).

Care of your rockery

Overwatering is rarely a problem with rockeries; both the shallowness of the container and its fast-draining soil usually prevent plants from becoming waterlogged. What you'll need to guard against is too *little* water. To keep plants from drying out, you may have to water frequently, even daily in warm weather.

These plants need just one annual application of a complete fertilizer in spring. Given too much, they'll grow tall and bushy.

In warm-weather climates, place a rock garden where it will soak up morning sun only. Where summers are milder, a rockery can safely sit in full sun all day long. No special wintertime protection is necessary—most of these plants are native to chilly parts of the globe.

Select plants carefully

At right, we list a selection of favorite plants for container rock gardens, focusing on readily available plants. For many enthusiasts, though, these close-up garden jewel boxes offer the perfect setting for a few especially prized plants

Against a backdrop of carefully positioned stone, pale-pink-flowered *Asperula gussonei* drapes gracefully over container edge.

such as the *Asperula gussonei* in the photograph above. Gems like this one are too rare to appear in most nurseries; you'll have to purchase them from a specialty nursery or order them through a catalog.

In addition to the plants listed below, smaller members of such well-known plant groups as *Dianthus* (pinks), *Primula* (primroses), and *Sempervivum* (hen and chickens) are excellent in container rock gardens. For the prettiest rockery, choose several kinds of plants.

Aethionema warleyense

Tiny, stiff gray leaves; bright pink alyssumlike flowers in early April.

Armeria
Sea pink, thrift

Leaves in compact tufts or rosettes; small white, pink, rose, or red flowers from early spring to late autumn.

Calluna vulgaris
Scotch heather

Foliage of green, yellow, chartreuse, gray, or russet often changes color in winter. Dwarf forms, just 2 to 4 inches tall, have white, pink, lavender, or purple flowers.

Festuca ovina glauca
Blue fescue

Single plants form small, exquisite clumps of blue gray grass.

Geranium sanguineum 'Prostratum'

Spreading, with roundish, medium green, finely cut leaves that turn blood red in autumn. Pure pink, five-petaled flowers from April to July.

Geum 'Borisii'

Foliage forms a 6-inch-tall mound; brilliant orange red flowers, borne on 1-foot spikes, bloom from spring through summer.

Helianthemum nummularium
Sunrose

Tiny, leathery, gray green leaves; multitudes of single or double inch-wide flowers in spring and summer, in white, pink, orange, red, apricot, or yellow. Spreads to 3 feet.

Origanum dictamnus
Crete dittany

Aromatic herb with slender, arching stems to 1 foot long and thick, roundish, woolly white leaves; produces pink to purplish flowers and rose purple fruit in conelike heads.

Perennials

Perennials differ from annuals in two obvious ways. First, they live from one year to the next when conditions are favorable. Second, most perennials don't bloom continuously from spring through summer; instead, they usually present a primary show of flowers in spring or summer, sometimes followed by a sequel of smaller blossoms (or a smaller quantity of blossoms) in summer or early autumn. In many cases, you can enhance this second wave of flowering by cutting or shearing plants back by one-half or more (see drawing at left) after the initial blooming period is over—always leaving a few inches of green, growing stems. Some perennials—especially autumn-blooming types such as asters and florist's chrysanthemums—typically have just one blooming period. Cut these back after flowering has ended to encourage abundant bloom the following year.

After blooms fade, cut back for more flowers.

As long as they receive good care, many perennials will survive indefinitely. They're often hardy plants: though top growth typically dies back to the soil surface during cold winters, roots remain alive. And in mild-winter areas (or when protected from frosts), many keep their foliage all year.

Since perennials live from year to year, it's not necessary to replant each spring (though some gardeners choose to do so). You'll need to repot a plant only when it becomes too large for its container.

Perennials are almost always started from transplants, only rarely from seed. You can safely move them at any time of year, but gardeners in cold-winter climates usually transplant in spring. Where winters are frost free, autumn is the most popular time to transplant. Just one plant will eventually spread to fill a medium to large container (see page 84)—but if you want to start out with a denser look, you can group three or four plants in each container (be prepared to move the "extras" to new pots in a year or so).

Agapanthus
Agapanthus, lily-of-the-Nile

Agapanthus blooms in summer and early autumn, producing magnificent, blue or white tubular, long-lasting flowers clustered atop tall stalks. Where winters are mild, its wide, strap-shaped leaves look stunning all year round.

You'll find many types of agapanthus available at your nursery. Flower stalks of standard-size varieties reach a height of 5 feet; those of dwarf forms grow only 1 to 2 feet tall. Most gardeners prefer dwarf forms such as 'Peter Pan' for container growing.

You can plant dwarf agapanthus at any time of year, though it's best to plant in spring. Allow one gallon-size plant to a medium-size container, two to a large container (see page 84). For a dramatic effect, put three or more standard-size plants in an extra-large container. Use a lightweight potting soil mix; keep soil moist, but not soggy. Be sure to provide protection from the hottest afternoon sun. From spring through summer, apply a complete fertilizer once a month. (Apply timed-release fertilizer less often, following package directions.)

Remove flower stalks after blooming, but don't cut leaves back. Where heavy frosts occur, protect this plant by moving it under an eave or into a greenhouse. Provide protection from slugs and snails (see page 109).

Aster
Michaelmas daisy

Pictured below and on page 8

This popular perennial is available in numerous species and hybrid forms; the most familiar is the autumn-blooming Michaelmas daisy (a hybrid of *Aster novae-angliae* and *A. novi-belgii*). Its blossoms are single or double, usually 1 to 2 inches across; they're borne on branching stems amid clumps of narrow leaves. *A. frikartii*, another popular aster, blooms almost all year in mild-winter areas if spent flowers are removed regularly.

You'll find both standard-size asters and dwarf forms. Standards range from 1 foot to over 4 feet in height; dwarfs grow from 1 to 1½ feet tall. Though dwarf asters better suit the size of most containers, taller types can be grown successfully in large planters (see page 84).

Set out aster transplants in late autumn or early spring, small transplants 4 to 6 inches apart, gallon-size plants one to a medium or large container (see page 84). Use a lightweight potting soil mix; keep soil moist, but not soggy. Apply a complete fertilizer once a month from spring through autumn (apply timed-release fertilizer less often, following package directions). For the loveliest flowers, grow asters in full sun. Divide clumps every year or two; in late autumn or early spring; discard old center.

Aster novi-belgii (New York aster)

Campanula isophylla
Campanula, Italian bellflower, star of Bethlehem

Pictured below right

Of the many varieties of *Campanula*, the trailing type—called Italian bellflower or star of Bethlehem—best suits container cultivation. From late summer through autumn, its 2-foot-long stems bear a profusion of star-shaped flowers, typically pale blue in color and about an inch wide. You'll also find other flower colors and sizes, though. The popular variety 'Alba' bears 1½ to 2-inch white blooms, and 'Maya' has soft gray leaves and large lavender flowers.

Trailing types of *Campanula* prosper in a lightweight potting soil mix. Space small transplants 4 to 6 inches apart, gallon-size plants one to a medium-size container (see page 84). Keep soil moist, but not soggy; from spring through autumn, apply a complete fertilizer once a month (apply timed-release fertilizer less often, following package directions). Place this perennial in partial shade or filtered sun. After the blooming period is over, cut plants back by about two-thirds. Protect from heavy frosts (see page 103).

Ceratostigma
Plumbago

Its bright blue phloxlike flowers have made *Ceratostigma* a very popular perennial. *C. griffithii* (Burmese plumbago) and *C. willmottianum* (Chinese plumbago) look alike: both have wiry stems, roundish 2-inch leaves of deep green, and vivid blue ½-inch flowers. Both reach a height of 2 to 4 feet; Burmese plumbago grows in a more compact shape. *C. plumbaginoides* (dwarf plumbago) resembles the first two types, but it's smaller, growing only 6 to 12 inches tall. All three species bloom from summer through autumn.

Plumbago spreads by underground runners and will fill a large pot in a year or so. Because of this, it's best planted by itself, one gallon-size plant to a medium or large container (see page 84).

Plant any plumbago in spring, summer, or early autumn, in a lightweight potting soil mix. Allow soil to dry out somewhat between waterings. From spring through summer, apply a complete fertilizer once a month (apply timed-release fertilizer less often, following package directions). Plumbago does best in full sun or partial shade. After the blooming period is over, cut back by one-half to two-thirds.

Chrysanthemum
Chrysanthemum, feverfew, marguerite, mum

Pictured on pages 6, 13, 14, 16, 25, 26, 28, 30

Many types of perennial *Chrysanthemum* are available. Perhaps the best-known container favorite is *Chrysanthemum morifolium*, the familiar florist's chrysanthemum. This plant blooms from late summer through autumn, offering a wide variety of flower shapes, sizes, and colors (every hue but blue). "Cushion" types (10 to 14 inches tall) are compact plants, densely covered with 2-inch blossoms during the blooming season. Large-flowered types look more dramatic—but they require frequent pinching (see page 104) during the growing season (until midsummer) to encourage bushiness and big blooms. Even after pinching, they often need staking. Cut back by one-half to two-thirds after the blooming season is over.

Many people use florist's chrysanthemums (in flower the year around) for quick color results indoors or out, simply disposing of the plants after the blossoms fade.

Another good container choice is the marguerite—*Chrysanthemum frutescens*. This fast-growing, shrubby perennial quickly forms a dense mass of coarsely cut green leaves; abundant white, yellow, cream, or pink flowers, single or double, bloom continuously during spring and summer.

If you don't control marguerite's growth, it can easily shoot up to a lanky 4 feet tall. To promote compact, attractively formed plants (about 1½ feet tall), you'll need to pinch growing tips often (see page 104). Or look for compact varieties (usually with smaller flowers) such as 'El Modeno Nays'. Where plants stay green through the winter, frequently cut them back by one-fourth to one-third to promote continued flowering. Cut back more heavily in early spring, but not to leafless wood.

Easy-to-grow *Chrysanthemum parthenium*, commonly called feverfew, forms fluffy clumps of finely cut foliage. In summer, its leafy stems, 2 to 3 feet long, bear large clusters of small white or yellow daisylike blossoms.

Plant chrysanthemum transplants in early spring, small transplants 4 to 6 inches apart, gallon-size plants one to a medium-size container (see page 84). All require a lightweight potting soil mix. Keep soil moist, but not soggy. During the growing season, apply a complete fertilizer once a month (apply timed-release fertilizer less often, following package directions). For best bloom, place chrysanthemums in full sun.

Delphinium
Delphinium

Delphinium has long been beloved for its spikes of violet blue flowers. Traditional types grow 3 to 6 feet tall—but newer, shorter varieties available today reach a height in containers of only 2 to 3 feet. These beauties are just the right size for containers. Look for 'Connecticut Yankee' and 'Blue Fountains'. The major flower show is in spring; secondary, smaller blooms appear in summer. Cut off spent flower spikes regularly to encourage continued bloom.

Plant delphinium transplants in early autumn, small transplants about 6 inches apart, gallon-size plants one to a medium-size container (see page 84). Use a lightweight potting soil mix, and keep it moist, but not soggy. From early spring through summer, apply a complete fertilizer once a month (apply timed-release fertilizer less often, following package directions).

Delphinium prefers full sun except in hot-summer areas, where a filtered-sun location is better. Slugs and snails may become a problem; see page 109 for methods of control.

Campanula isophylla (Italian bellflower)

Digitalis
Foxglove

Pictured on pages 3, 8

Many gardeners don't think of fox-gloves as container plants—prob-ably because, at one time, only very tall types (to 6 feet or more) were available. But 2 to 3-foot dwarf forms are on the market today, and they make a stunning container dis-play. Look for such named strains as 'Foxy', 'Excelsior', and 'Glox-iniiflora', and for particular species such as *Digitalis grandiflora* and *D. mertonensis.*

Most foxglove types offer flowers in shades of purple, lilac, rose, pink, cream, and yellow. The main bloom-ing season comes in mid and late spring; secondary, smaller flowers appear in summer.

In early autumn, plant trans-plants in a lightweight potting soil mix, small transplants about 6 inches apart, gallon-size plants one to a medium-size container (see page 84). Keep soil moist, but not soggy.

From early spring through early summer, apply a complete fertilizer once a month (apply timed-release fertilizer less often, following pack-age directions). Give foxgloves par-tial shade or filtered sun. Regularly cut off spent flower spikes to stimu-late new flowering stems.

Euryops
Golden shrub daisy

Pictured on pages 7, 16

Closely resembling marguerite (*Chry-santhemum frutescens*, page 41), golden shrub daisy grows from 2 to 6 feet tall. Several types are available; all have finely cut silvery green leaves and quantities of bright yellow daisylike flowers. The primary bloom comes in late winter and spring (throughout spring in cold-winter climates), followed by scattered flow-ers during the rest of the year.

Set out transplants in spring. Space small transplants about 6 inches apart; allow one gallon-size plant to a medium-size container, two to a large container, and three to an extra-large container (see page 84). Use a lightweight potting soil mix or a blend of half garden loam, half potting mix. Allow soil to dry out somewhat between waterings. From spring through summer, apply a complete fertilizer monthly (apply timed-release fertilizer less often, fol-lowing package directions). Golden shrub daisies do best in a full-sun location. Cut back by one-third to one-half after the major blooming period is over.

These are tough, tolerant plants. They often last several years, taking on an almost Oriental look as their trunks become exposed.

Gerbera jamesonii (Gerber daisy) and *Felicia amelloides* (blue marguerite)

Felicia amelloides
Blue marguerite

Pictured below left and on page 6

Like the marguerite (*Chrysanthe-mum frutescens*, page 41), *Felicia amelloides* has yellow-centered daisylike blooms—but *Felicia's* flowers are pale blue, rather than marguerite's typical white, yellow, or pink. The cheery blossoms appear in profusion on dense-foliaged, mound-ing plants up to 2 feet tall. Summer is the main blooming season, but where winters are frost free, you can expect scattered bloom throughout the year. (In cold-winter areas, blue marguerite is usually treated as an annual.)

Set out transplants in spring, one gallon-size plant to a medium-size container (see page 84). Use a light-weight potting soil mix; let soil dry out somewhat between waterings. From spring through summer, apply a complete fertilizer once a month (apply timed-release fertilizer less often, following package directions). Place plants in a full-sun location. After the main blooming period ends, cut plants back by one-third to one-half.

Gerbera jamesonii
Gerber daisy, Transvaal daisy

Pictured at left and on page 12

If ever there was an elegant daisy, this Transvaal beauty is it. Showing off beautiful colors and exquisite form, the 3 to 4-inch blooms are borne singly atop 1½-foot stems. (A much smaller variety called 'Happy Pot' is well suited to containers.)

Flower colors range from cream and yellow to coral, orange, and red. The major show of flowers comes in early summer and late autumn.

Plant Transvaal daisies in spring, small transplants about 6 inches apart, gallon-size plants one to a medium-size container (see page

84). Use a lightweight potting soil mix enriched with extra peat moss (one-third to one-half the total con-tainer volume). Keep soil moist, but not soggy.

From spring through early au-tumn, apply a complete fertilizer at one-half the recommended monthly amount every 2 weeks. (Apply timed-release fertilizer less often, following package directions.) These plants prefer full sun, but they'll also toler-ate partial shade. Regularly remove spent blossoms.

When frost threatens, move Trans-vaal daisies to a greenhouse or bury them 6 inches deep in a mulch in a cold frame. Or bring them indoors; placed in a sunny window, they'll stay green all winter, and may even bloom.

Hosta
Funkia, hosta, plantain lily

Hosta is known more for its large, decorative leaves than for its less significant flowers. Shaped like elon-gated hearts or pointed ovals, the leaves may be solid green, steel blue, chartreuse, or two shades of green; some are centered with white or bor-dered or variegated in white or cream. Leaves arise directly from the ground on leaf stalks of different lengths. You'll find hosta in sizes from 4-inch miniatures to 2-foot-tall clumps that spread 5 feet across.

Plant transplants in spring, one gallon-size plant to a medium-size container, one 5-gallon-size plant to a large or extra-large container (see page 84). Use a lightweight potting soil mix; keep soil moist, but not soggy. From spring through summer, apply a complete fertilizer once a month (apply timed-release fertilizer less often, following package direc-tions). Give hosta full or partial shade except in cool or humid cli-mates, where a full-sun location is best. This plant goes dormant in winter; move container to an out-of-the-way spot until growth resumes in spring.

Lavandula angustifolia
English lavender

If you love fragrant plants, lavender is a perfect choice for your container garden: during the blooming season in mid to late summer, this old-fashioned favorite fills the air with spicy, delicious perfume. (Its foliage is fragrant, too.) Slender spikes of long-lasting lavender flowers emerge from clumps of finely cut gray green leaves. Standard-size plants range from 1 to 4 feet tall and just as wide, but dwarf forms (1 to 2 feet tall) are best for containers. Look for such named varieties as 'Compacta', 'Hidcote', 'Munstead', and 'Twickel Purple'.

Plant lavender transplants in spring, one gallon-size plant to a medium-size container (see page 84). Use a lightweight potting soil mix; allow it to dry out almost completely between waterings. Apply a complete fertilizer only once or twice during the spring-through-summer growing season. Lavender does best in full sun.

To keep plants compact and neat, cut back plant by as much as half immediately after blooming (don't expect much second bloom).

Limonium
Sea lavender, statice

A perennial that's sometimes grown as an annual, statice produces airy clusters of rose or lavender flowers atop 2-foot stems that rise from clumps of leathery, rounded leaves.

Spring is the usual planting season for statice—but where winters are frost free, you can also plant in autumn. Set out transplants in a lightweight potting soil mix, spacing them about 8 inches apart (or sow seeds, then thin seedlings).

Allow soil to dry out somewhat between waterings. From spring through summer, apply a complete fertilizer once a month (apply timed-release fertilizer less often, following package directions). Statice needs full sun.

Lotus berthelotii
Parrot's beak

This trailing plant's common name describes its flowers—inch-long scarlet blooms that resemble a parrot's beak. Foliage is fine textured and silvery gray. Parrot's beak looks most striking in tall containers or hanging baskets. Expect the major show of flowers in summer; cut plants back after they flower for abundant bloom the following year.

This plant does best in areas where winters are frost free. In cold-winter areas, protect it as you would a Transvaal daisy (*Gerbera jamesonii*, facing page).

Plant parrot's beak transplants in spring, one gallon-size plant to a medium-size container (see page 84). Use a lightweight potting soil mix, and allow it to dry out somewhat between waterings. From spring through summer, apply a complete fertilizer once a month (apply timed-release fertilizer less often, following package directions). Parrot's beak does best in a full-sun location.

Oenothera
Evening primrose

This easy-to-grow plant produces pleasantly scented 3 to 5-inch flowers in summer. The delicate-looking blossoms have yellow and white centers; petals are usually yellow, sometimes pink. Evening primrose grows 10 inches to 2 feet tall and has narrow, velvety, gray green leaves.

Set out transplants in early autumn, one gallon-size plant to a medium-size container (see page 84). This plant does fine in a lightweight potting soil mix; allow soil to dry out somewhat between waterings. From spring through summer, apply a complete fertilizer once a month (apply timed-release fertilizer less often, following package directions). Give full sun.

Cut back halfway after initial bloom; more flowers may follow in late summer or early autumn.

Pelargonium
Geranium, pelargonium

Pictured below and on pages 1, 4, 5, 6, 7, 8, 14, 16, 22, 26, 28

Geraniums are an all-time container favorite—they produce vivid flowers for months on end, and they're easy to care for. Their use as year-round outdoor perennials is limited to areas with mild (frost-free) winters, but all geraniums grown in containers can spend winters indoors.

Shrubby Martha Washington or Lady Washington types (*Pelargonium domesticum*) grow to 3 feet or more. Their tooth-edged leaves are rounded to heart-shaped; round, ruffly flowers, up to 2 inches across, bloom in clusters during spring and summer. Flower colors include white, pink, red, purple, and lavender; the petals of some are marked with darker blotches.

Common or garden geraniums (*P. hortorum*) are shrubby plants that reach a height of about 3 feet. They have soft, hairy leaves and stems. The single or double flowers are smaller than those of Martha Washington geraniums—but flower clusters are often larger and fuller. Common geraniums bloom continuously from spring through autumn, offering blossoms in white, pink, salmon, orange, red, or purple.

Ivy geraniums (*P. peltatum*) are trailing plants; their thick, glossy leaves resemble those of ivy. The inch-wide single or double flowers grow in clusters; colors include white, lavender, pink, and rose.

Scented geraniums are grown for their fragrant leaves; choose from scents such as rose, peppermint, citrus, apple, and coconut.

Plant all types of geraniums in spring. Space transplants from 4-inch pots 6 to 8 inches apart, gallon-size plants one to a medium-size container (see page 84). Use a lightweight potting soil mix. Water generously, then let soil dry out somewhat before you water again. From spring through summer, apply a complete fertilizer just once every 2 months. Where summers are hot (and especially where they're both hot and dry), give plants filtered sun, partial shade, or full shade during the hottest part of the day.

To promote bushiness, pinch off growing tips periodically. In frost-free climates, where geraniums can persist outdoors as perennials, prune them at least halfway back in late winter or early spring, just before the growing season begins. Elsewhere, cut back by one-third to one-half after the blooming period is over (in summer or autumn).

Pelargonium hortorum (common geranium), mint-rose scented geranium

Penstemon gloxinioides
Beard tongue, penstemon

For container gardening, choose the new hybrid forms of penstemon. These grow 2 to 4 feet tall, producing narrow, pointed leaves and spikes of trumpet-shaped flowers. Flower color ranges from pale pink to red and purple; petals are often marked with darker colors. Spring is the main blooming season; a second bloom usually follows in summer or autumn. These plants may be treated as annuals in cold-winter areas.

Plant penstemon transplants in early autumn in mild climates, spring in cold climates. Space small transplants about 6 inches apart, gallon-size plants one to a medium-size container (see page 84). Use a lightweight potting soil mix, and keep it moist, but not soggy. During the growing season, apply a complete fertilizer once a month (apply timed-release fertilizer less often, following package directions). Penstemon needs full sun—but where summers are hot and dry, it's best to place it in partial shade or filtered sun.

After the initial blooming period, cut penstemon back halfway.

Primula
Primrose

Pictured below and on pages 16, 20, 23

Of literally hundreds of types of primroses, the following four are both commonly available and easy to grow in containers: *Primula polyantha* (English primrose or polyanthus primrose), *P. malacoides* (fairy or baby primrose), *P. obconica*, and *P. juliae* (Juliana hybrids).

Where spring weather is cool, primroses will bloom almost continuously in spring. (Where winters are frost free, they often blossom in late winter and very early spring.) You'll find flowers in subtle pastels as well as in brilliant shades of red, blue, yellow, gold, and purple.

English primroses are exceptionally sturdy plants, growing 6 to 7 inches across. Their dark green leaves resemble those of romaine lettuce. Vivid clusters of 1 to 2-inch flowers, borne on stout 10 to 12-inch stalks, come in red, blue, yellow, orange, bronze, white, and several pastel shades. Each blossom sports a small yellow "eye" at the center. In mild climates, English primroses bloom continuously throughout the year if faded flowers are removed.

For a more delicate and lacy look, choose fairy (baby) primroses. Each plant forms a 6 to 8-inch-wide rosette of pale green leaves with ruffled edges. Slender 10 to 12-inch stalks rise from rosette centers, carrying tiers of tiny white, pink, rose, red, or lavender blooms. Despite their fragile look, plants stand up well under rain and wind. Though technically perennials, fairy primroses aren't as sturdy as other primroses; they're usually treated like annuals and pulled up after bloom.

Ball-like clusters of large flowers topping 12 to 14-inch stalks distinguish the *P. obconica* primroses. Plants grow 8 to 10 inches across; they have large, rounded leaves and showy white, pink, lavender, or purple blooms.

The Juliana primroses are prized for the miniature foliage that covers their 6-inch span. Their rounded bouquets of bright 2 to 3-inch blooms top 3 to 4-inch stalks.

Plant primrose transplants in a lightweight potting soil mix in any size container, spacing plants 4 to 8 inches apart. Where winters are frost free, plant primroses in autumn for winter bloom, or in winter for very early spring bloom. In cold-winter areas, plant them in early spring for spring and early summer color.

Keep soil moist, but not soggy. Every 2 weeks, from spring through summer, apply a complete fertilizer at half the recommended monthly amount. (If you use a timed-release fertilizer, you won't need to apply it as often; follow package directions.)

Plants do best in partial shade, with protection from hot afternoon sun. Cut off spent blossoms regularly.

Snails, slugs, and spider mites may cause problems; see page 109 for ways to control these pests. Leaf miners attack *P. obconica*; control them by spraying affected plants with diazinon.

Senecio cineraria
Dusty miller

Pictured below and on page 26

Famous for its mounds of woolly white foliage, dusty miller produces 2-foot-long, tongue-shaped leaves, each cut into many blunt-tipped lobes. It forms a clump about 2 feet high and just as wide. Yellow flowers appear sporadically during the year—but since their color clashes with the foliage, some people cut the flower spikes off before the blossoms open.

In spring, plant dusty miller transplants in a lightweight potting soil mix or in a blend of half garden loam, half potting mix. Space small transplants 4 to 6 inches apart, gallon-size or larger plants one to a medium-size container (see page 84). Allow soil to dry out somewhat between waterings. From spring through summer, apply a complete fertilizer once a month (apply timed-release fertilizer less often, following package directions). Dusty miller prefers full sun.

Clockwise, from top left: *Primula polyantha* (English primrose), *P. malacoides* (fairy primrose), *P. obconica*, *P. juliae* (Juliana hybrids)

Senecio cineraria (dusty miller)

Container water gardens

Cool, tranquil water, shimmering in a garden pool, seems to wash away cares and tension. To bring water-garden refreshment to your container collection, you'll need only a few springtime hours and a few simple ingredients: a suitable container, a sunny site, gallons of water, some bog or aquatic plants (you may have to order these ahead from a specialty catalog), and a few water snails and goldfish to help keep the pool clean.

The container. If you want a good-size water garden, buy a 25-gallon (at least) container; almost any leakproof vessel of the appropriate capacity will do. A half barrel is an attractive choice, and it's easy to find. For a more ornate pool, use a large decorative ceramic tub, such as the one shown in the photo at right. It's best to select a container without drainage holes; if holes are present, be sure to plug them tightly before filling the container with water.

The site. Because a water-filled 25-gallon container is heavy (over 200 pounds), it makes good sense to set up your water garden in its permanent location. You may prefer to place it on garden ground rather than on a deck or patio: the pool will have to be drained and scrubbed once a year, and there's always some chance of seepage.

As you evaluate possible sites, remember that it's important to provide plenty of sunshine: most aquatic plants need at least 6 hours of full sun daily. Keep in mind, too, that your water garden should complement its surroundings; you may want to locate the pool where it will reflect color from blooming trees and flowers, for example.

Filling & planting. Before placing a half barrel in its permanent position, fill it with water; then stir in a cupful of lime (sold at nurseries) to neutralize the acids in the wood. Let the filled barrel sit for several days. Then empty it, move it to its permanent site, and refill it. Let the water stand for a week before planting.

With the exception of plants which simply float freely on the water's surface, aquatic plants must be potted before being placed in the pool. Plastic pots are best, since they hold up better than clay when submerged in water. Fill pots with garden loam; an inch-thick layer of sand at the top of each pot helps keep soil particles in place.

Submerge planted pots in the pool, usually positioning them so pot tops are 6 inches or more under water. A few plants do best if pots are only partially submerged; see the following entries. To raise plants to the proper height, you'll need to set up pedestals made from bricks or overturned pots on the pool's bottom.

Add a goldfish or two to keep the water free of insects; don't overfeed fish, since this could disturb the pool's ecological balance. A few water snails help keep the pool clean by nibbling algae and decaying matter.

Once a year, drain the pool and scrub it out thoroughly with a mixture of four parts water to one part household bleach.

Possible plants. Listed below are a few popular water plants.

Cyperus alternifolius
Umbrella plant

Spreading leaves radiate like ribs of an umbrella at tops of 2 to 4-foot stems (a dwarf form is also avail-

In sylvan setting, water garden features Japanese iris at left, slender dwarf cattail (*Typha angustifolia*) at right, and, floating on the surface, water hyacinth.

able). In cold weather, move indoors to a well-lighted room (will survive out of water).

Cyperus isocladus
Dwarf papyrus

Long, narrow leaves and flowers are borne in filmy brown and green clusters atop slender 1½-foot stems.

Eichhornia crassipes
Water hyacinth

Hollow-stemmed plant with broad, nearly circular floating leaves. Bears violet flowers with yellow eyes. Needs warmth to flower profusely.

Equisetum hyemale
Horsetail

Bright green, rushlike hollow stems have distinctive black and ash-colored rings at joints. Submerge pot about halfway to rim.

Iris ensata
Japanese iris

Velvety blooms—pinks to purples and white, often with contrasting edges—amid sword-shaped foliage. Plant rhizomes 2 inches deep; submerge pot halfway to rim.

Nymphaea
Water lily

Round, floating leaves, medium to dark green, showy flowers of yellow, red, pink, copper, or white. Store and replant tropical types each year in all but mildest climates.

Sagittaria latifolia
Arrowhead

Spikes of white flowers; dark green, arching, arrow-shaped leaves. Submerge so pot top is 12 to 14 inches below surface.

Bulbs

Beautiful and easy to grow, bulbs in containers provide color indoors or out. Keep blooming season in mind when you choose bulbs—if you select an assortment with successive blooming periods, you can treat yourself to a nonstop flower show from early spring right through summer and into autumn.

Bulbs such as amaryllis (*Hippeastrum*) and clivia are quite content to take up permanent residence in containers, producing splendid

For massed bloom, plant with sides almost touching.

Cover pots to keep bulbs cool and shaded.

blooms year after year. But other types—crocus, hyacinth, iris, and tulip—usually provide just one unforgettable season of container bloom; the next year, flowers are likely to be smaller and fewer. Many gardeners prefer to move these types from containers to garden flower beds after the first year (in the open ground, they'll often continue to bloom profusely).

Many of the plants we describe in this section grow from true bulbs; others sprout from similar structures such as corms, rhizomes, tubers, and tuberous roots. All these plants go through a dormant period, when their leaves wither and die back to the soil surface. Active growth resumes in spring or summer, fueled by food stored in the bulb or bulblike structure. This stored food is manufactured in the leaves, so it's important to keep them green and healthy after the plant has flowered if you want the bulb to bloom again. Let the leaves keep growing until they turn yellow and wither.

Always buy the best bulbs available, usually graded Number 1. They may cost slightly more, but their improved performance more than compensates for the higher price. Plant bulbs as soon as possible after they appear for sale in nursery or catalog—usually in autumn for spring-flowering bulbs, in late winter or early spring for summer and autumn-blooming types.

Crocus ancyrensis (yellow crocus)

Many bulbs need cold temperatures during part of their dormant period if they're to bloom. Where winters are frost free, refrigerate the bulbs before planting.

Almost all bulbs grow best in a loose, fibrous planting mix of equal parts garden loam, coarse sand, and organic matter such as peat moss, leaf mold, or ground bark. Commercially available packaged lightweight potting soil mix provides the right balance; before you plant, add 2 tablespoons of steamed bonemeal to each 16-inch pot (adjust amount up or down for larger or smaller pots).

Plant large spring-flowering bulbs with their tips (pointed ends) level with the soil surface; small bulbs should sit 1 to 2 inches below the surface. For a massed "bouquet" effect, set bulbs close together, sides almost touching (see drawing at left). Settle additional soil mix firmly around bulbs; then water well, filling containers to the rim two or three times to ensure that soil mix is thoroughly damp.

While roots are forming, you'll need to keep soil cool to prevent premature sprouting. Place containers in a cool, dark spot—under a tree or in a shady spot on the north side of the house. Where winters are warm, some special insulation is necessary: after setting containers in a cool, shaded location, cover them with 3 to 4 inches of peat moss, wood shavings, branches, sawdust, or sand (see drawing at left).

After about 8 weeks, check a few pots, looking for roots in the drain holes and leaf tips poking through the soil. When such signs appear, place containers in a sunny spot where top growth can develop and turn green; then begin normal watering.

Begonia tuberhybrida
Tuberous begonia

Pictured on page 17

Hybrid tuberous begonias bloom all summer long, offering flowers in a variety of forms and vivid colors. You'll find both single blossoms and ruffly double blooms resembling roses or carnations, all in white and shades of yellow, orange, red, and pink. Sometimes a contrasting color appears on petal edges. Plant form varies, too; there are dramatic upright types as well as cascading varieties such as *Begonia tuberhybrida* 'Pendula'. These plants are so spectacular that some gardeners become collectors.

Tubers are sold in January and February, when pink growth buds first appear on them. Plant in coarse leaf mold, buds facing up; sprinkle just enough leaf mold over tubers to barely cover them. Tubers will sprout very quickly. Two to three weeks later, when plants are about 3 inches tall, transplant to pots or hanging baskets. One plant will grow to fill a small to medium-size pot; if you want a lusher effect, group two or three in a large container (see page 84). If you're using hanging baskets, choose wooden ones—moisture-loving tuberous begonias do well in cedar or redwood, both of which retain moisture well. (Or use wire baskets lined with sphagnum moss—see page 23).

Fill containers with coarse leaf mold or peat moss; then set plants just deep enough to barely cover tubers. Place in partial shade; keep soil moist, but not soggy. From spring through summer, apply a complete fertilizer once a month (apply timed-release fertilizer less often, following package directions).

When leaves begin to yellow and wilt, reduce water, allowing soil to dry out. After stems have naturally fallen off plants, lift tubers from soil, shake off, and dry in the sun for 3 days. Then store in mesh bags in a cool, dry place until growth buds appear again in spring.

Clivia miniata
Kaffir lily

Kaffir lily's clusters of brilliant orange and yellow funnel-shaped flowers rise from dense clumps of long, dark green leaves. Bloom is heaviest during March and April, but the first flowers may appear many months before then—sometimes as early as December. Ornamental red berries appear after flowering ends.

Kaffir lily bulbs are only rarely available in their dormant state, but you can purchase (and plant) the started lilies the year around. Set each plant in a medium-size container (see page 84) filled with a rich soil mix (the kind sold for African violets or orchids is good). While plant is actively growing—from late winter until the end of summer—keep soil moist, but not soggy. From spring through summer, apply a complete fertilizer once a month (apply timed-release fertilizer less often, following package directions).

Bring Kaffir lily inside before the first autumn frosts. Cut down on water and let plant rest in a cool location until late winter; then move to a bright, warm window. Resume normal watering when flower stalk is 6 inches tall. As soon as weather warms in spring, return lily to a bright spot outside.

Crocus
Crocus

Pictured on facing page

These small flowers of white, vivid yellow, or violet are one of the first signs of spring in many places (in cold-winter regions, they may even bloom through the snow). Crocuses look especially attractive when mass-planted (with sides of corms almost touching) in shallow containers; they'll flower for 2 to 3 weeks.

In autumn, plant crocus corms—pointed end up and 2 inches deep—in containers filled with a light-weight potting soil mix. Starting when first top growth appears in early spring, water enough to keep soil barely damp; place containers in full or filtered sun. (It's not necessary to fertilize.)

After flowers fade, allow foliage to die back naturally. Then store pots in a cool, dry place until planting time.

Container-grown crocuses are often disappointing the second year; you may prefer to transplant bulbs to the garden rather than trying for a second season of container bloom.

Cyclamen
Cyclamen

Pictured below and on pages 7, 10, 16, 29

Cyclamen's delicate, long-stemmed flowers stand tall above rounded, often variegated leaves. Pink, white, red, or rose-colored petals curve elegantly, giving blossoms the look of shooting stars. The blooming period covers 4 to 8 weeks—from mid or late winter to early spring in mild-winter regions, from mid to late spring where winters are cold.

Plant cyclamen tubers during their dormant period (June through August), one to a small container (see page 84). Fill containers with a lightweight potting soil mix—or better yet, a mix of half peat moss, half soil mix. Then set in tubers so the top half of each is visible above the soil surface (tuber top is studded with small growth buds). Place in a filtered-sun location and keep soil barely moist until growth begins in autumn (in mild-winter climates) or early spring (in cold-winter areas). Then move to a spot receiving partial shade or morning sun only.

Starting when spring bloom fades, apply a complete fertilizer once a month until the growing season ends in summer. (Apply timed-release fertilizer less often, following package directions.) When leaves start to wither, stop fertilizer. Reduce water, giving only enough to keep soil barely damp, and move containers to a filtered-sun location. Return to a spot receiving partial shade when growth resumes the following year.

Cyclamen (cyclamen)

Dahlia
Dahlia

Pictured on page 8

Dahlias are available in a parade of colors: yellow, orange, red, pink, lavender, and white. Blossoms may be single or double; some have fluffy golden yellow centers. Dwarf and intermediate types are best for containers, since they don't require pinching or staking. (These two types grow to 1 and 1½ feet tall, respectively.)

For bloom from June or July to mid-autumn, plant tuberous roots in spring; allow one tuberous root or cluster to a 10-inch pot, three to a 15-inch pot. Fill pots with a lightweight potting soil mix. Then bury roots with sprout side up, about 3 to

Freesia (freesia)

5 inches deep. Place pots in a cool, dark place until shoots appear; water just enough to keep soil barely moist.

When growth begins, move pots to a sunny location. Keep soil moist, but not soggy. When you water, avoid wetting the foliage—it's vulnerable to mildew. (If plants develop mildew despite all precautions, check page 108 for methods of control.) From the time top growth is active through autumn, apply a complete fertilizer monthly. (Apply timed-release fertilizer less often, following package directions.) Reduce watering after flowering stops in autumn, allowing soil to dry out entirely. When most of the foliage is dry, cut stems off a few inches above the ground. Lift tubers from pots and store them in a cool, dry place, covered with sawdust or similar insulating material, until planting time the following spring.

Endymion
Bluebell

These dainty springtime flowers of brilliant blue, pink, purple, or white add a sparkling accent to a mixed container planting. The small bell-shaped blossoms are borne on leafless 4 to 12-inch stalks.

In autumn, plant bluebell bulbs points up and about 2 inches deep, in pots filled with a lightweight potting soil mix. (A 6-inch pot holds six bulbs.) Keep in a cool, dark place until bulbs sprout; then move to a full-sun location to encourage abundant bloom. Keep soil moist, but not soggy.

After blooming ends in early spring, apply a complete fertilizer (one application is all that's necessary). Continue to water normally until foliage begins to wither in early summer; then cut down on water, allowing soil to dry out completely. When foliage is dry and brown, lift bulbs from soil, place in mesh bags, and store in a cool, dry place until planting time.

Freesia
Freesia

Pictured below left

Their clear colors and enchanting fragrance make freesias a pleasing addition to a container garden. From just one package of corms, you'll usually get blossoms in a mixture of colors: white, pink, rose, purple, orange, and yellow. Flowers bloom in spring, clustered atop 1 to 1½-foot stems; they're typically single, 1 to 1½ inches across. If you'd like larger blooms (to 2 inches across) or double-petaled types, look for Dutch hybrid freesias (now available at many nurseries).

Pots of freesia in bloom can be brought indoors for a few days for a special treat. Their heady fragrance will fill a room in a few hours.

In autumn, plant freesia corms 1½ to 2 inches deep, pointed end up, in a container filled with a lightweight potting soil mix. For a full display, evenly space approximately one dozen corms in an 8-inch pot. Place in a shady location and keep soil damp and cool.

Soon after shoots emerge in early spring, move pot to a sunny spot. Apply a complete fertilizer just once, after flowering ends in spring. After foliage dies back in early summer, store pot in a cool, dry place until the following autumn. Then resume watering until the growth cycle ends.

Hippeastrum
Amaryllis

Amaryllis blooms over a 2 to 4-week period, flaunting enormous flowers (8 to 9 inches across) atop thick stems that can grow as tall as 3 feet. Flower color ranges from white to delicate shell pink to blazing red; some bicolors are available, as are variously marked and striped plants. This is a popular bulb to force for Christmas bloom—specially pre-

pared bulbs are available in most nurseries in autumn. If planted indoors on November 1, such bulbs have an excellent chance of blooming by Christmas. Bulbs not forced for Christmas can be planted any time they're available—usually from autumn through early spring.

One of this bulb's most endearing traits is its willingness to bloom year after year, given only the modest care described below. And unlike many more exotic bulbs, amaryllis tends to bloom more profusely (and sometimes even produce larger blossoms) with each successive year.

When you're ready to plant amaryllis, check the bulb's roots and remove any that are obviously damaged or dead. Then select a pot that's large enough to allow an inch of growing space all around sides of bulb; a 4-inch bulb needs a 6-inch pot, for example.

Fill pot to within an inch of its rim with a lightweight potting soil mix; then plant bulb so tapered upper half is exposed to the air. Soak soil thoroughly and move pot to a bright, warm room. Keep soil barely moist until growth begins. After sprouting, increase water, but still allow soil to dry out somewhat between waterings.

Flower stalk and leaves may appear simultaneously or consecutively (leaves almost immediately after flower stalk). Cut off stalk after blossoms have faded; then, as leaf growth becomes active, apply a complete fertilizer at half the recommended monthly amount every 2 weeks. (Apply timed-release fertilizer less often, following package directions.) The greater the number of healthy leaves your bulb produces, the finer its flowers in the next blooming period.

When leaves begin to turn yellow, gradually withhold water, stop fertilizer, and let bulb go dormant. Store it (still in its pot) in a garage or basement until the following late autumn or early winter; then start it into growth again by watering. (Leave the bulb in the same soil, or repot it if you wish. If you repot, discard any dead or damaged roots.)

Hyacinthus orientalis
Hyacinth

Pictured below

This richly fragrant flowering bulb is an excellent choice for all climates. Its exquisite springtime spikes of bell-shaped flowers, 8 to 18 inches tall, are available in red, purple, blue, cream, and white; individual blossoms last for 2 weeks or longer. Flower spike size is directly proportional to bulb size—so for the largest spikes, purchase the biggest bulbs you can find.

For spring bloom, plant hyacinth bulbs in autumn. Use a shallow container (4 to 6 inches deep) filled with a lightweight potting soil mix. Set bulbs into container pointed end up, placing them close together (sides almost touching); then barely cover with soil mix. After shoots emerge, place container in a full-sun location. While plants are in leaf, keep soil moist, but not soggy.

If you intend to keep bulbs for planting the following year, apply a complete fertilizer once a month from spring through summer, starting when flowers fade. (Apply timed-release fertilizer less often, following package directions.) Withhold water in late summer, allowing foliage to wither naturally. Then lift bulbs from soil and store them in mesh bags in a cool, dry place until planting time.

Since container-grown hyacinths tend to blossom rather sparsely (or not at all) the second year, you may prefer to transplant bulbs to garden flower beds rather than trying for a second season of container bloom.

Hyacinthus orientalis (Dutch hyacinth)

Iris
Dutch iris, English iris, Wedgwood iris

Bulbous iris make showy, graceful additions to a container garden. Dutch, English, Spanish, and Wedgwood types adapt particularly well to medium-size flowerpots; for smaller containers, choose *Iris reticulata* and its varieties or *I. danfordiae*. Bulbous iris bloom for several weeks in spring and early summer, offering almost every possible flower color (only true green and true red are missing).

Plant iris bulbs in late autumn—six to eight to an 8-inch pot, pointed end up and 1 to 2 inches deep. Use a lightweight potting soil mix, and keep it just barely damp until roots form. When roots and shoots appear, move pots to a full-sun location; begin watering more heavily, keeping soil moist, but not soggy.

Starting after flowering ends and continuing through summer, apply a complete fertilizer once a month (apply timed-release fertilizer less often, following package directions). Taper off watering in late summer, allowing foliage to wither naturally. Then move pots to a cool, dark spot; begin watering lightly again in late autumn.

Since container-grown iris don't usually flower well the second year, you may prefer to plant bulbs in garden flower beds rather than trying for a second season of container bloom.

Lilium
Lily

These colorful bulbs thrive in the confined growing space of a container. In fact, many gardeners who have never been able to grow lilies successfully in the garden have had considerable luck with lilies in containers.

Lilies are happiest in big pots, since sizable containers most easily provide the perfect drainage they need. Excellent choices include 'Enchantment', *Lilium henryi* hybrids, *L. longiflorum* and its hybrids, and *L. speciosum* and its hybrids. All stand 2 to 3 feet tall and bloom in late spring or summer. Bulbs are usually available for early spring planting.

In general, lilies require 1) a standard lightweight potting soil mix; 2) ample moisture throughout the year; and 3) shade at the roots and filtered sun for blooming tops (if you can't provide this kind of light, give plants a full-sun location that's protected from the hottest afternoon rays).

Lilies also need pots that are roomy enough to drain perfectly. For a single lily bulb, use a deep 5 to 7-inch pot. For more bulbs, select fairly straight-sided pots, at least 12 inches deep and 15 inches across. Pots this size can hold quite a large volume of soil—enough to keep roots cool and moist without constant attention from the gardener. After filling pot one-third full of soil mix, gently set in bulbs, roots spread out and pointing downward. Cover with about one inch of soil mix. Allow three to ten bulbs per container (the more bulbs, the more impressive the display of blossoms). Water thoroughly to settle soil mix.

While roots are getting established, keep pot in a cool, shady spot; water just enough to keep soil barely moist. Move pot to a sunny location after shoots emerge; as they approach blooming size (about 2 feet), increase water, keeping soil moist, but not soggy. To increase the number of buds the following year, apply a low-nitrogen fertilizer (such as 5-10-10) soon after leaves appear, then again 6 weeks later.

When bloom is finished, taper off watering—but don't allow soil to dry out entirely, even after top growth has completely died back. Keep pot in a protected area, such as under an eave, while bulbs are dormant. Begin normal watering again when weather warms up in spring.

Narcissus
Daffodil, narcissus

Pictured below

Daffodils and other *Narcissus* are probably the most popular of all spring-flowering bulbs—as well as the easiest to grow. Their familiar blooms, solid or bicolored, come in white, cream, and dazzlingly bright shades of yellow, orange, and pink. For continuous bloom from December to April, plant early and late varieties in October and November, respectively. (Early-blooming types flower from December to February, late bloomers from February to April.)

Plant bulbs, pointed end up and sides almost touching, in a container filled with a lightweight potting soil mix. (A 12-inch pot holds 10 to 12 bulbs.) Cover bulbs with an inch or two of soil, then water to dampen and settle soil. Store in a cool, dark

Clockwise from top left: *Narcissus* 'Twink', 'Golden Eagle', 'Yellow Cheerfulness', and 'Windblown'

place for 8 to 10 weeks, or until roots grow and look well formed (to see them, peer into pot's drain hole or carefully tip soil mass from pot).

Once roots have formed, move container to a warm, sunny spot. Keep soil moist, but not soggy; apply a complete fertilizer monthly from the time flowers fade in spring until foliage begins to wither in summer. (Apply timed-release fertilizer less often, following package directions.)

After flowers fade, begin monthly applications of a complete fertilizer. When foliage begins to yellow and wither in summer, stop fertilizer and cut back on water; move pots to a cool, dry place. In autumn, soak soil thoroughly once; then keep barely moist until roots form.

Container-grown *Narcissus* are often disappointing the second year; you may prefer to transplant these bulbs to garden flower beds rather than trying for a second season of container bloom. Their first bloom season in the garden won't match their container display, but from the second year onward they should put on a good show.

Ranunculus asiaticus
Ranunculus

Looking something like brilliantly colorful, jumbo-size balls of petals, ranunculus bloom in pure yellow, orange, pink, red, cream, and white. Masses of blossoms open in spring, borne atop 1½ to 2-foot stems. These make lovely cut flowers.

Ranunculus are usually started from tubers, though seeds and small transplants are occasionally available. Plant the clawlike tubers in late autumn or early spring (they're hard as rock, so soak them in lukewarm water for several hours before planting). Use a container that's at least a foot in diameter. After filling container with a lightweight potting soil mix, set in tubers—"claws" down, 2 to 3 inches apart and 1 inch deep. (A 12-inch pot will hold 20 to 24

small tubers.) Place in a cool, dark spot until roots are established; keep soil just barely moist.

After young plants are 3 to 4 inches tall, move container to a sunny location. Water regularly, keeping soil moist, but not soggy. There's no need to fertilize.

Ranunculus tubers are very short lived; most gardeners discard each year's tubers after plants die back. Snails and birds love to eat ranunculus shoots as they emerge from the soil. See page 109 for methods of controlling snails; to foil birds, cover containers with wire mesh (see drawing on page 108).

Tulipa
Tulip

Pictured below and on pages 11, 16, 28

Tulips grow beautifully in pots, at least for the first year—in subsequent years, though, they may prove disappointing. But there are definite advantages to growing these familiar flowers in containers. For one thing, a group of a few dozen tulips massed together in one container usually makes a more stunning display than

the same number planted in the ground. And certain varieties with unusual colors or shapes (such as Rembrandt, Parrot, and Peony-flowered strains) are more effectively shown off in their own containers than in mixed flower beds.

Plant tulip bulbs in autumn, setting them close together—nearly touching each other—with their tips just below the soil surface. (In mild-winter areas, bulbs may have to be refrigerated for a few weeks prior to planting; ask at your nursery.) Use a lightweight potting soil mix. Water thoroughly at planting time; set pots in a cool, shaded area and keep soil cool and moist until roots and shoots appear. Then move pots to a sunny spot. Increase water to keep soil moist, but not soggy.

As soon as flowering is over, begin a fertilizing program: every 2 weeks, apply a complete fertilizer at half the recommended monthly amount. Stop fertilizing in midsummer when foliage begins to yellow and wither, signaling the end of the growing season. Also begin withholding water at this point, allowing soil to dry out entirely. Once foliage has turned brown, remove bulbs from soil, place them in mesh bags, and store in a cool, dry place until planting time in autumn.

Tulipa (tulip)

Vines

Wandering far and wide, climbing up or cascading down, vines don't seem compatible, at first, with container confinement. Yet as long as they receive good care, many will thrive in pots for quite some time.

Their looks alone are certainly reason enough to include vines in your container garden. But remember, too, that potted vines can provide the perfect solution when you need to bring a little leafy softness to a bare expanse of wall or fence. They're also ideal for portable garden screens: simply attach a sturdy trellis to the outside of the container (see drawing at left) or insert one inside before planting.

Attach trellis to train vine for garden screen.

Some vines have attaching devices such as tiny suckers, rootlets, tendrils, and twining stems. These plants easily cling by themselves to whatever support you provide, be it trellis, fence post, wire, or brick wall. But other vines, lacking "grippers" of their own, need a little help from you. To train them, tie them to the support with raffia, soft twine, or reinforced paper ties from the supermarket. For heavy-stemmed vines, use something stronger — clothesline, for example. Some vines, such as wisteria, can be trained into tree form.

As a rule, it's easiest to start vines from the 1 to 2-year-old plants sold at nurseries in gallon cans, though you can begin with smaller transplants if you prefer. (In some cases, nursery transplants are unavailable; you'll have to start these varieties from seed.) For container cultivation, avoid fast-growing, fiercely clinging types such as honeysuckle and trumpet vine.

All vines will do well in a lightweight potting soil mix. Keep soil moist, but not soggy. During the spring-through-summer growing season, pinch back (see page 104) and train new growth diligently to keep vines looking lush and tidy. Also during this time, treat your plants to regular doses of a complete fertilizer. For spring or summer-planted vines, wait 2 weeks before the first application; for those planted in autumn or winter, hold off on fertilizer until spring.

Bougainvillea
Bougainvillea

Pictured below and on pages 7, 21, 30

Vibrant and tropical looking, bougainvillea produces summertime blooms in white and shades of red, magenta, rose, purple, orange, and pink. The colored "petals" are really large bracts (modified leaves); the true flowers, surrounded by the bracts, are hardly noticeable.

Because bougainvillea's colors are so vivid, it can clash with other flowering plants—so be sure to locate your vine where it will enhance surrounding plantings. (Vines in one-gallon cans are often in bloom when you buy them.)

Bougainvillea is evergreen where winters are frost free, but in less temperate climates it's generally treated as an annual. To protect it from frost, place container under an eave or in a greenhouse when weather cools. If the vine survives one or two cold winters, it will do without any special treatment in moderately cold weather.

Choose a low-growing, shrubby type such as 'Hawaii' or 'La Jolla' for a large container (see page 84) or hanging basket; it will provide you with lush, dense foliage as well as bright blooms. Though a typical vining bougainvillea will reach a height of 15 or more feet, it can be kept smaller with pruning (see pages 104 to 106). For upward growth, bougainvillea must be tied in place. For longest possible growing season, plant in early spring as soon as all danger of frost is past.

Bougainvillea's roots don't knit together in a firm root ball as do those of most plants—so when you plant, use the following method to avoid damaging roots. To begin with, purchase a vine in a metal can. Then fill the new container with a lightweight potting soil mix and hollow out a planting hole. Place metal nursery can in hole and slit can side to its base in four to six places. Pull side sections away from roots and fill in with soil, leaving can in place. Or cut out can bottom, leaving sides intact, and plant (a metal can will eventually rust away).

Keep soil moist, but not soggy; in midsummer, allow it to dry out somewhat between waterings. From spring through summer, apply a complete fertilizer once a month. (Apply timed-release fertilizer less often, following package directions.) Give full sun except in hot-summer areas, where partial shade is better.

Prune heavily in spring after frost, at other times of year to encourage new growth, or to shape or direct growth (see pages 104 to 106).

Bougainvillea (bougainvillea)

Clematis
Clematis

Thick-foliaged clematis is among the most beautiful of all flowering vines. It adapts well to container life; once established, it blooms profusely and lives for a long time, reaching a height of 6 to 20 feet. It clings to a support without tying.

For container gardening, choose one of the named hybrid varieties of deciduous clematis. Other types, such as evergreen *Clematis armandii*, are too rampant for successful container growing.

Numerous named hybrids are available, offering large six-petaled flowers in pure white, blue, purple, red, rose, pink, lavender, and yellow (the colorful "petals" are actually sepals). Some varieties bloom only in spring; others flower once in spring, then again in summer.

Nurseries offer clematis in cans for planting at almost any time of year, but if you buy the vine in spring or summer you can see the color of the flowers. Plant in a container that's at least 16 inches deep. Use a lightweight potting soil mix, covering root ball with 2 inches of soil. Apply a mulch to surface.

Keep soil moist, but not soggy. From spring through summer, apply a complete fertilizer once a month (apply timed-release fertilizer less often, following package directions). Give clematis filtered sun.

Cobaea scandens
Cup-and-saucer vine

A vigorous, beautifully flowering perennial (sensitive to frost; frequently grown as an annual), cup-and-saucer vine grows to 20 feet or more. Its tendrils will grasp almost any surface for support. Dangling, bell-shaped flowers are green when they first open, turning to rosy purple a bit later on. They bloom from spring until autumn on graceful foot-long stems.

Start seeds indoors in early spring. Or wait until all danger of frost is past, then sow directly into a large container (see page 84) filled with a lightweight potting soil mix. Thin seedlings according to directions on seed packet.

Keep soil moist, but not soggy. From spring through summer, apply a complete fertilizer once a month (apply timed-release fertilizer less often, following package directions). Place in full sun. In cold weather, protect from frosts by moving container under an eave or into a greenhouse. Cut back at this time.

Fatshedera lizei
Tree ivy

Its common name, tree ivy, gives a fair description of this plant's appearance. It's a shrubby, evergreen vine that produces thick ivylike leaves, 8 inches across. (Flowers are insignificant.) Tree ivy does not cling to surfaces on its own; it needs to be tied to a sturdy support such as a trellis to keep it upright. With such support, it will grow as tall as a small tree (to 5 feet or more).

You can plant tree ivy at almost any time of year. Transplant the vine from its nursery can into a medium to large container (see page 84) filled with a lightweight potting soil mix. Keep soil moist, but not soggy. From spring through summer, apply a complete fertilizer once a month (apply timed-release fertilizer less often, following package directions). Place in a spot receiving filtered sun or partial shade, sheltered from drying winds.

If growth gets out of hand in early spring (before new growth starts), pinch growing tips to encourage side branching. Or prune back almost to the "crown"—the top of the root ball, right above ground level. (See pages 104 to 106 for pruning pointers.)

Hedera helix
English ivy

Pictured at left and on pages 9, 12, 16, 18

This familiar, dependable vine produces neat evergreen foliage. There are literally dozens of named varieties of *Hedera helix*; depending on the type, leaves are pure green or variegated, lobed or pointed. Ivy does tend to be invasive, but you needn't worry about this characteristic when you grow the vine in the confines of a container. Train the small-leaved kinds along almost any surface or onto a wire form or trellis; they'll climb about as high as the support is tall. Ivy is also very attractive combined with colorful annuals in hanging baskets.

You can plant ivy at almost any time of year. Transplant the vine from its nursery can into a medium-size container (see page 84) filled with a lightweight potting soil mix. Keep soil moist, but not soggy; never let it dry out completely between waterings. From spring to early autumn, apply a complete fertilizer once a month (apply timed-release fertilizer less often, following package directions). Ivy grows well in full sun (protected from the hottest afternoon rays) or partial shade.

Kadsura japonica
Scarlet kadsura

Changing its appearance with the seasons, scarlet kadsura offers fresh green foliage in spring, white flowers in summer, reddish leaves in autumn—and scarlet berries in winter, if you have both male and female plants. This evergreen perennial is a fast-growing vine that can twine as far as 15 feet. Plant small nursery transplants at the base of a sturdy support, or train vines up a tall trellis or arbor. No ties are needed.

Plant scarlet kadsura at almost any time of year, using a medium to large container (see page 84) filled with a lightweight potting soil mix. Keep soil moist, but not soggy. Once every 2 months, from spring through summer, apply a complete fertilizer. Scarlet kadsura thrives in full sun except in the hottest areas, where partial shade is best. Prune vines for shape in early spring before new growth starts (see pages 104 to 106).

Hedera helix (English ivy)

Lantana
Lantana

Valued for its generous show of color over a long season (every month of the year in frost-free areas), fast-growing lantana is a shrubby vine that twines from 3 to 6 feet. It's usually treated as an annual in cold-winter climates, but in more moderate regions it's a perennial. Its small clusters of flowers bloom in vivid shades of yellow, orange, pink, lavender, cerise, purple, and cream.

This vine doesn't climb well, but it makes a lush cascading plant for a container suspended from a hook or placed on a tall support. You could also tie it to a sturdy trellis or other support.

In spring, move the vine from its nursery can into a medium-size container (see page 84) filled with a lightweight potting soil mix. Allow soil to dry out almost completely between waterings. Every 2 months, from spring through summer, apply a complete fertilizer. Lantana needs a hot, full-sun location; it mildews if kept in a shady spot.

Phaseolus coccineus
Scarlet runner bean

Scarlet runner bean is the perfect way to provide a shady screen in hot summer weather. These fast-growing vines readily attach themselves to strings suspended from an overhang and attached to the side of their planter. They'll easily clamber up 10 to 12 feet. Slender clusters of cheery red flowers appear in late spring and early summer, followed by dark seed pods—tasty when young and small, but tough later on. Beans can be shelled from older pods for cooking like green limas.

Plant seeds in late spring, in a large container (see page 84) that's at least 1 foot deep. Thin seedlings according to seed packet directions. Use a lightweight potting soil mix; keep soil moist, but not soggy. Starting when plants are about 1 foot tall and continuing until the end of summer, apply a complete fertilizer every 2 months. Scarlet runner bean does best in full sun.

This vine is an annual, so you'll have to replant it yearly.

Thunbergia alata
Black-eyed Susan vine

Pictured below left

Twining for 3 feet or more in one season, black-eyed Susan vine looks especially dramatic when spilling from a hanging basket. Its short, tubular blossoms come in shades of orange, yellow, buff, and white, all with distinctive black centers. Heaviest bloom is in midspring, but flowers appear intermittently during the other warm months as well. This vine will survive the winter indoors.

Black-eyed Susan vine transplants are occasionally available in nurseries, but most gardeners start this plant from seed. In spring, sow seeds in a large container (see page 84) filled with a lightweight potting soil mix; thin seedlings to 1 foot apart when they're 1 to 2 inches tall. Keep soil moist, but not soggy. From spring through summer, apply a complete fertilizer once a month (apply timed-release fertilizer less often, following package directions). Give full sun or partial shade.

Tropaeolum
Canary-bird flower, nasturtium

Pictured on page 24

Two different vining forms of *Tropaeolum* are available—*T. majus* (the common nasturtium) and *T. peregrinum*, commonly called canary-bird flower.

T. majus, a vigorous annual, bears abundant blooms in shades of yellow, orange, red brown, rose, and cream. Quite easy to grow from seed, it will trail or climb to 6 feet or more if tied to adequate support; the semi-trailing type extends 2 to 6 feet. (A bush form of *T. majus* is also available; see page 38.)

Also easy to start from seed, the annual canary-bird flower quickly grows into a rugged vine covered with fringed yellow flowers. When given support for its twining stalks, it can reach 10 feet or more.

Follow planting, watering, and fertilizing directions given on page 38 for *Tropaeolum majus*. Common nasturtium prefers full sun; canary-bird flower, partial shade.

Thunbergia alata (black-eyed Susan vine)

Trachelospermum jasminoides
Star jasmine

Pictured on pages 1, 13

This widely grown evergreen vine is popular for its neat, glossy foliage and for the clusters of tiny, heavily fragrant flowers it bears from spring through summer. Tied along a support, it will extend to 20 feet.

You can plant star jasmine at almost any time of year. Move the vine from its nursery can into a medium-size container (see page 84) filled with a lightweight potting soil mix. Keep soil moist, but not soggy. From spring through early autumn, apply a complete fertilizer once a month (apply timed-release fertilizer less often, following package directions). Star jasmine grows in partial shade or full sun (provide protection from hottest afternoon rays).

Wisteria
Wisteria

Pictured on page 54

Famous for the long, fragrant clusters of purple or white flowers it produces in spring, wisteria often lives to a great age. This deciduous vine grows well in a container; it readily attaches itself to any kind of strong support, growing as tall (or as long) as the support. With considerable pruning, you can grow it as a small "tree" (see page 106).

Plant wisteria at any time of year. Move the vine from its nursery can into a large or extra-large container (see page 84) filled with a lightweight potting soil mix. Keep soil moist, but not soggy. From spring through summer, apply a complete fertilizer every 2 months. Wisteria prefers full sun.

Bonsai, ancient container art

Tiny Chinese wisteria (*Wisteria sinensis*) blooms beautifully. A bonsai's size gives no clue to age: this one's 25 years old.

A centuries-old Japanese art, *bonsai* is like sculpture that uses woody plants as the raw material.

In this small space, we can give only the briefest discussion of traditional bonsai techniques. For more information, consult the *Sunset* book *Bonsai, Illustrated Guide to an Ancient Art.*

Choosing & planting

In addition to bonsai classics such as pines, maples, and junipers, there's no reason not to cultivate many other trees, shrubs, and woody vines—and even shrubby herbs—in the same manner.

Any simple container that enhances the plant's character will serve, though classic Japanese bonsai pots look the most appropriate.

For an excellent all-purpose bonsai soil mix, combine equal parts leaf mold, garden loam, and river or quarry sand (don't use beach sand; the salt it contains is harmful to plants). Fill the pot, position the plant firmly with its crown at the soil level, and water gently.

Shaping a bonsai

A bonsai's severely restricted root space helps inhibit its growth and keep it tiny. Pruning and pinching are used not only to hold the plant to a miniature size, but to mold it into the desired shape.

The first shaping step comes at planting time. If the foliage is too thick, obscuring the plant's basic shape, the artist thins it out. Next comes a single major pruning—usually done during the winter following planting, when the plant is well established and dormant.

The following spring or summer (for deciduous plants) or autumn or winter (for evergreens), when the plant's wood is relatively pliable, the artist may gently bend the branches to refine shaping. Wire (such as plastic-covered No. 10 or 16 house wire) is wrapped in even coils around each branch. This wire bracing is removed a year or two later.

Periodic nipping and pinching shape the plant further and keep its growth in check (deciduous plants require such maintenance more often than evergreens do). See pages 104 to 106 for details.

Care of a bonsai

Learn your own bonsai's water needs by poking your finger an inch or two into its soil to check for dryness. Most bonsai need frequent watering, from twice daily (morning and evening) in hot weather to three times a week in cooler conditions.

It's best to use rain water or distilled water, since chemically treated tap water may harm the plant. Pour the water into a watering can with a fine-spray spout; then let it stand for a day, preferably in the sun, before watering. As you water, imitate a light rainfall over the foliage.

Wait 4 to 5 weeks after planting before applying fertilizer. Then apply a complete liquid fertilizer, diluted to one-quarter the recommended monthly amount, every 2 weeks from spring through summer. During very hot weather, omit fertilizer for a month or two.

Though a bonsai likes plenty of sunshine, it needs protection from the strongest summer rays. Shelter it from heavy rains and harsh winds, as well. (But don't bring it inside the house—it won't do well.) Give the pot a quarter turn every now and then to encourage even growth. The plant may need repotting after a few years; see page 97.

Favorite plants

The plants listed below are especially good choices for bonsai.

Acer
Maple

All members of this group are excellent for bonsai. Japanese maple is one of the best: graceful form, deeply lobed leaves that are crimson in autumn. See page 63.

Camellia
Sasanqua types

Varying from bushy and upright to spreading and vinelike; bushy types with small leaves are best for bonsai. Abundant flowers in pink, rose, red, or white, autumn through winter. See page 56.

Cotoneaster

Arching, small-leafed branches take well to shaping. White to pinkish spring flowers are followed by red berries in autumn. See page 56.

Juniperus
Juniper

Many types of evergreen shrubs with needlelike or scale-like foliage. Can be trained to resemble much older miniature conifers. See page 58.

Pinus
Pine

Very large group; choose shorter-needled types such as *P. contorta* (shore pine). See page 66.

Punica
Pomegranate

Most varieties produce fruit in late autumn. Very showy: leaves are bronzy when young, bright green or golden green in summer, yellow in autumn. See page 81.

Rhododendron
Kurume-type azaleas

Compact, twiggy, thick-foliaged shrubs with small leaves; profusion of springtime blossoms in pink, salmon, red, or orange. See page 61.

Wisteria

Adaptable vines with lovely flower clusters. Stake vertical stems; pinch or prune out tips. See page 53 and photo above.

Shrubs

Versatile and varied, tubbed shrubs enhance any garden. Many offer a different look for each season, brightening the garden with changing leaf color, showy flowers, and colorful berries. Others, by virtue of striking shape or dramatic foliage, look like stunning outdoor sculptures.

Even "ordinary" shrubs such as firethorn (*Pyracantha*) and India hawthorn (*Raphiolepis*), which seldom inspire a second glance when mass-planted in the garden, can look quite exciting if set off in the right container. And all the evergreen shrubs in this section provide a rich, textured background for blooming annuals and perennials. Many shrubs have dwarf counterparts (often with *"nana"* in their botanical names) that are well suited for containers.

Beware of sharp edges when pulling can apart.

Though slow-growing shrubs naturally last longest in containers, almost any shrub can tolerate container life for many years. Start out with a container that's a few inches larger all around than the can or pot that carried the shrub home from the nursery. If you wish to keep a shrub at a particular size or shape, give it a periodic pruning, following the guidelines on pages 104 to 106.

You can plant shrubs at almost any time of year, though it's best to plant in spring in cold-winter areas, in early autumn in mild-winter regions. Many of these plants are happiest in a standard lightweight potting soil mix; others can tolerate a heavier mixture of half garden loam, half potting mix. A few (camellias, for example) need acid soil mix (see page 95).

Nurseries frequently sell shrubs in metal or plastic containers. Have metal cans split before leaving the nursery (see drawing above). Use caution with sharp can edges.

In general, shrubs need a monthly application of a complete fertilizer throughout their growing season (spring through summer). If you plant your shrubs in spring or summer, let them settle in for 2 weeks before the first fertilizing (autumn and winter-planted shrubs should receive no fertilizer until the spring following planting).

Aucuba japonica
Japanese aucuba

Pictured below

Glossy, tooth-edged leaves make Japanese aucuba an attractive container choice. Several types are available; depending on the variety, foliage may be solid green, variegated, or spotted. If you have both male and female plants, the females will produce a brilliant autumn show of red berries.

This is a good-size shrub: if not pruned, it can grow 6 feet tall (or taller) and just as wide.

You can plant Japanese aucuba at almost any time of year. Follow the planting guidelines on pages 96 to 97, using a large or extra-large container (see page 84) filled with a lightweight potting soil mix. Keep soil moist, but not soggy, while shrub is young; once it's established (after the first year), allow soil to dry out somewhat between waterings. From spring through summer, apply a complete fertilizer every 2 months. Place in a location receiving full or partial shade.

Bambusa
Bamboo

Pictured on page 14

Unlike "running" types of bamboo, which spread with alarming speed, *Bambusa* grows into a bushy clump that expands slowly.

Many types of *Bambusa* can stay outside during cold weather; nursery personnel can tell you if the type you select is frost tolerant. But all these plants—however tolerant of frost they are—take nicely to a winter spent indoors. Given plenty of light and good air circulation, they'll get along quite comfortably.

Plant bamboo at almost any time of year, following the guidelines on pages 96 to 97. Use a large (at least 16 inches across) or extra-large container (see page 84), filled with a mix of half lightweight potting soil mix, half garden loam. Keep soil moist, but not soggy. From spring through summer, apply a complete fertilizer monthly (apply timed-release fertilizer less often, following package directions). Place in full sun or partial shade.

Aucuba japonica (Japanese aucuba)

Brunfelsia pauciflora
Yesterday-today-and-tomorrow

Handsome, dark-green-foliaged *Brunfelsia pauciflora* grows upright to about 3 feet. In areas where winter weather is very mild, it's evergreen; elsewhere, it loses most of its leaves with the autumn frosts. This shrub is prized primarily for its 2-inch-wide flowers, appearing in clusters in spring and early summer. The blossoms are purple when they open, turn to lavender the next day, white the day after that—a fascinating progression that inspires the plant's common name.

Plant this shrub at almost any time of year, following the guidelines on pages 96 to 97. Use a medium to large container (see page 84) filled with an acid soil mix (see page 95). Keep soil moist, but not soggy. From spring through summer, apply an acid fertilizer (see page 102) monthly. This shrub performs best in partial shade (be sure to protect it from hottest afternoon sun).

For a spectacular but heavy hanging pot, plant *Brunsfelsia pauciflora* in a 12-inch or larger container, then weight or tie down limbs to make them trail over the sides.

Buxus
Box, boxwood

Pictured on page 9

Slow uniform growth and compact arrangement of small, shiny evergreen leaves have made boxwood a container favorite for centuries. It's renowned for its ability to live in the same container for many years without repotting. Boxwood's natural shape is upright and somewhat billowy, but it's often sheared into neat cubes, spheres or other formal shapes. Left unpruned, this shrub may reach a height of 4 to 20 feet, depending on the variety. All types readily accept repeated pruning to a desired size or shape (see pages 104 to 106).

Plant boxwood at almost any time of year, following the guidelines on pages 96 to 97. Use a medium to large container (see page 84) filled with a lightweight potting soil mix or a blend of half garden loam, half potting soil mix. Allow soil to dry out somewhat between waterings. From spring through summer, apply a complete fertilizer every 2 months. Place container in full sun or partial shade. Boxwood is sometimes attacked by spider mites or scale insects; see pages 108 and 109.

Camellia
Camellia

Pictured below left

It's easy to see why camellias are such popular shrubs. Their glossy evergreen foliage is handsome all year round; their spectacular flowers brighten the cooler months. You'll find countless sizes and varieties of this shrub, all offering flowers in white and shades of red and pink (some types have variegated blooms). In fact, there are so many varieties that it's a good idea to take several trips to the nursery during the December-through-May blooming season, just to see what's available.

Many gardeners favor *Camellia japonica*. In containers, it's usually seen as a 6 to 12-foot shrub with a 3 to 6-foot spread. Delicate *C. sasanqua* and showy *C. reticulata* are also worthy container subjects. The former is most often seen in containers at 6 to 8 feet tall. Some Sasanqua forms trail and cascade; others have lightly fragrant flowers. *C. reticulata* grows to 10 feet tall and almost as wide in containers. It has some of the biggest and most spectacular flowers of all camellias.

The usual planting time for camellias is winter through spring; follow the guidelines on page 96 to 97. Fill planting containers with an acid soil mix (see page 95). When planting, keep trunk base just above soil line. As a general rule, plant a gallon-can camellia in a 12 to 14-inch-wide tub, a 5-gallon-size plant in a 16 to 18-inch tub.

Keep soil consistently moist, but never let it become soggy. A thick organic mulch helps to keep roots cool and moist. When the blooming period is over, begin applications of an acid fertilizer (choose one that's specially formulated for camellias—see page 102), following label directions carefully for timing and amounts.

Camellias do best in partial shade or in a spot receiving morning sun only. In cold-winter climates, they may need some overhead protection; place containers under an eave or other overhang (see page 103).

Cotoneaster
Cotoneaster

A good candidate for a tubbed espalier (see page 105) or natural screen, rock cotoneaster (*Cotoneaster horizontalis*) puts forth angled, spreading branches. It reaches a height of 2 to 3 feet and will spread 6 to 8 feet unless pruned (see pages 104 to 105). *C. congestus* is a low, ground-hugging form; it grows slowly, eventually attaining a height of 1 to 1½ feet and a width of about 3 feet. Both species have small evergreen leaves, whitish flowers, and red autumn berries; both thrive in hot or cold climates.

Plant cotoneaster at almost any time of year, following the guidelines on pages 96 to 97. Use a large container (see page 84) filled with a lightweight potting soil mix. Allow soil to dry out somewhat between waterings. From spring through summer, apply a complete fertilizer once every 2 months (apply timed-release fertilizer less often, following package directions). Cotoneaster prefers full sun, but it will tolerate partial shade.

Daphne odora
Winter daphne

Growing up to 4 feet tall and just as wide, this compact shrub is well worth the slight extra care it demands. It's good looking the year around—but especially in early spring, when it delights gardeners with clusters of exquisitely scented blossoms. Some types have white flowers; others have pink to deep red blooms with creamy pink throats.

Plant winter daphne at almost any time of year, following the guidelines on pages 96 to 97. Use a large container (see page 84) filled with a mix of one part garden loam, one part fine sand (not beach sand), and two parts ground bark. Take care not to overwater—allow soil to

Camellia (camellia)

dry out almost completely between waterings. As soon as the blooming period is over, apply a dose of complete fertilizer; continue to apply once a month until the end of summer. (Apply timed-release fertilizer less often, following package directions.) Place plant where it will receive cool morning sun and at least 3 hours of afternoon shade each day (hot afternoon rays can .damage winter daphne).

Elaeagnus pungens
Silverberry

This tough evergreen shrub is as easy to grow as it is to admire. Tiny, fragile spring or summer flowers, nestled in silvery leaves, precede dry, silvery berries in winter. (Birds enjoy snacking on the berries, but don't try eating them yourself.) There also are named selections that have foliage variegated or margined with yellow or silvery white. Silverberry can reach a height of 8 feet or more in a container, making it ideal for use as a screen. It tolerates seaside conditions well.

Fuchsia hybrida (fuchsia)

Plant silverberry at almost any time of year, following the guidelines on pages 96 to 97. Use a large container (see page 84) filled with a lightweight potting soil mix. Allow soil to dry out somewhat between waterings. From spring through summer, apply a complete fertilizer once a month (apply timed-release fertilizer less often, following package directions). Silverberry likes full sun.

Escallonia
Escallonia

Glossy evergreen foliage and clusters of pink, red, or white flowers characterize this large group of plants. The blooming season is at its peak in summer and autumn—but where the climate is mild, you can expect some flowers almost all year round.

Newer named hybrid varieties of escallonia are best for containers; they usually have a more compact form (3 to 6 feet tall) and bloom more abundantly than older types. The new dwarfs *Escallonia* 'Newport Pink' and *E.* 'Teri' are especially appealing choices.

Plant escallonia at almost any time of year, one to a medium to large container (see page 84); follow the planting guidelines on pages 96 to 97. Use a lightweight potting soil mix, and allow it to dry out somewhat between waterings. From spring through summer, apply a complete fertilizer once a month (apply timed-release fertilizer less often, following package directions). Escallonia tolerates full sun in mild-summer areas, but prefers filtered sun or partial shade where summers are hot.

Fatsia japonica
Japanese aralia

Japanese aralia's dark green, deeply lobed leaves are big (up to 16 inches across) and glossy, clustering toward branch tips on plants that may reach a height and width of 6 feet or more.

You can plant this shrub at almost any time of year. Following the guidelines on pages 96 to 97, transplant shrub from its nursery can into a large container (see page 84) filled with a lightweight potting soil mix. Keep soil moist, but not soggy. From spring through summer, apply a complete fertilizer once a month (apply timed-release fertilizer less often, following package directions).

Japanese aralia prefers a shady location, though it will take much sun where summers are cool. In cold-winter climates, it may need to be brought indoors for protection from frost.

Fuchsia
Fuchsia

Pictured at left and on pages 2, 6, 16

Fuchsias have long been prized for the lovely blossoms that dangle gracefully from their arching stems. You'll find flowers in showy shades of pink, red, and violet, as well as in combinations of these colors. Flowers

come in a variety of sizes; they aren't scented, but their nectar attracts hummingbirds.

Dozens of named varieties are available—enough to keep any collector happy for a lifetime. Choose upright types for boxes and tubs, trailing forms for hanging baskets.

Plant fuchsias in spring or summer, one to a medium-size container (see page 84). Follow the planting guidelines on pages 96 to 97. Use a lightweight potting soil mix; keep soil moist, but not soggy. Be especially attentive to watering in warm weather, giving plants a drink twice a day if necessary. In hot-summer climates, plants will appreciate daily misting or sprinkling to increase humidity.

Every 2 weeks, from spring through summer, apply a mild complete fertilizer (such as liquid fish emulsion) at half the recommended monthly amount. (If you're using a timed-release fertilizer, you won't need to apply it as often; follow package directions.)

Fuchsias thrive in a cool, shady garden nook—under a patio overhang, for example. They prefer a mild summer climate, so be sure to protect them from wind and hot sun. In frost-free areas, they can spend the winter outdoors; prune them in spring (see pages 104 to 106), cutting back to within two buds of the previous summer's growth.

Where winters are cold, move your fuchsias to a protected area such as an unheated garage or basement and mulch heavily. When weather warms in spring and all danger of frost is past, cut back to live wood by carefully removing dry, twiggy growth. (In regions where winters are severe and protection isn't practical, treat fuchsias as annuals, replanting each year.)

Early symptoms of attack by fuchsia mites include curled, puckered, and distorted new growth; as damage progresses, leaves, stems, and flowers become blistered, swollen, and malformed. Treat by removing mite-damaged foliage and spraying with diazinon, kelthane, orthene, or orthenex.

Gardenia
Gardenia

Famous for their richly perfumed, waxy white flowers, gardenias also boast glossy bright green foliage. The best-known variety, *Gardenia jasminoides* 'Mystery', grows 4 to 5 feet tall; it has large double flowers. *G. j.* 'Veitchii', a compact 3-foot plant, offers abundant inch-wide blooms. Both types bloom all summer long. *G. j.* 'Radicans', 6 to 12 inches tall and spreading 2 to 3 feet, is especially attractive when spilling over the sides of a hanging basket.

Plant gardenias at almost any time of year, following the guidelines on pages 96 to 97. For each plant, use a large container (see page 84) filled with an acid soil mix (see page 95). When planting, keep crown (top of root ball) slightly above soil level. Keep soil moist, but not soggy. From spring through summer, apply an acid fertilizer (see page 102) every 3 to 4 weeks (apply timed-release fertilizer less often, following package directions).

In mild climates, gardenias thrive in full sun; but where summers get hot, they do better with filtered afternoon sun.

Juniperus (juniper)

Hydrangea
Hydrangea

Pictured on page 17

For a look of lush floral abundance, nothing beats a summertime show of hydrangeas massed on a deck or patio. Their 12 to 16-inch flower clusters range from white through shades of blue, purple, pink, and red.

Plant hydrangeas at almost any time of year, following the guidelines on pages 96 to 97. Set each plant in a large or extra-large container (see page 84) filled with a mix of half lightweight potting soil mix, half peat moss. Give these shrubs plenty of water during summer, but don't let soil get soggy. From spring through summer, apply a complete fertilizer every 6 weeks. Be sure to shelter plants from hot afternoon sun. To get the biggest flower clusters, reduce the number of stems. Prune to control size and form (see pages 104 to 106).

To achieve blue flowers on pink and red varieties and to keep blue-flowered kinds from changing hue, treat soil with a solution of aluminum sulfate (1 tablespoon in a gallon of water). Make monthly applications two or three times before the April-to-June blooming season.

Ilex
Holly

With or without its traditional red berries, holly makes a happy addition to any garden, especially at holiday time. If you want berries, you'll usually need to grow both male and female plants (the female bears the fruit). Chinese holly (*Ilex cornuta*) is an exception; it's a self-pollinating type that produces exceptionally large berries. A number of named varieties are sold, varying in height from 18 inches to 10 feet, and in spininess of leaves. Taller Chinese hollies will grow 6 to 8 feet tall in a container. English holly (*I. aquifolium*) is the traditional Christmas holly, reaching a height of 6 to 10 feet in a container. Most hollies are content to live in the same container for many years, without repotting.

You can plant holly at almost any time of year. Follow the general guidelines on pages 96 to 97, using a large container (see page 84) filled with a mix of half lightweight potting soil mix, half peat moss. Keep soil moist, but not soggy. From spring through summer, apply a complete fertilizer once a month (apply timed-release fertilizer less often, following package directions). Holly performs well both in sunny spots and in partial shade.

Juniperus
Juniper

Pictured at left and on page 6

Picturesque in both branch and trunk, juniper assumes sizes and shapes to suit nearly any container need. More than 100 types are commonly available, from ground-hugging to upright and tall—with every possible variation in between. There's a wide range of foliage colors, as well.

Juniper is a cold-tolerant shrub that responds well to pruning and shaping. Some of the lower-growing, compact forms of juniper make good bonsai subjects (see page 54).

Plant juniper at almost any time of year. Follow the general guidelines on pages 96 to 97, using a large or extra-large container (see page 84) filled with a mix of half lightweight potting soil mix, half garden loam. Allow soil to dry out somewhat between waterings. Every 2 months, from spring through summer, apply a complete fertilizer. Grow in full sun or partial shade.

Lagerstroemia indica
Crape myrtle

Crape myrtle is available in three sizes. Standard (single-stem) types, growing 8 to 15 feet tall, resemble small trees. Shrub forms reach 5 to 7 feet; miniatures are just 2 feet tall (they're a good choice for hanging baskets). All three sizes offer clusters of crêpe-paper-like blossoms in white and shades of pink, red, and purple. The blooming season is a long one, beginning in May or June and lasting right up to the first autumn frost (until late October in frost-free areas). In autumn, leaves turn to brilliant gold, orange, or red. After leaves fall in winter, the shiny pink bark becomes visible.

Summer is the best time to select a crape myrtle for planting—since it's in bloom then, you can choose just the flower color you want. Plant according to the guidelines on pages 96 to 97, using a large or extra-large container (see page 84) for a standard or shrub-type plant.

Fill container with a lightweight potting soil mix; keep soil moist, but not soggy. From spring until early autumn, apply a complete fertilizer monthly (apply timed-release fertilizer less often, following package directions). Crape myrtle can survive hot, dry conditions and thrives in full sun (newer miniatures also accept partial shade). Powdery mildew (see page 108) is a problem in cool-summer areas.

Ligustrum
Privet

Pictured on page 9

A number of kinds of privet are available; all are excellent container choices. Like boxwood (page 56), many types can be clipped into various formal shapes. Since trimming removes most of the flower-bearing branches, clipped shrubs bloom sparsely or not at all—but untrimmed privet produces abundant, showy clusters of white flowers with a noticeable fragrance in late spring or early summer. Berrylike blue black fruit follows the blossoms.

You can plant privet at almost any time of year. It's available in nursery cans the year around; in some regions, you'll find bare-root shrubs in winter and early spring. Follow the planting guidelines on pages 96 to 97, using a large or extra-large container (see page 84) for each shrub. Fill containers with a mix of half lightweight potting soil mix, half garden loam; keep soil moist, but not soggy. From spring through summer, apply a complete fertilizer once a month (apply timed-release fertilizer less often, following package directions). Give privet full sun or partial shade.

Magnolia
Saucer magnolia, star magnolia, tulip tree

For striking springtime bloom, choose one of these deciduous shrubs. *Magnolia soulangiana* is called saucer magnolia or tulip tree: it produces saucer-size, tuliplike blooms up to 6 inches across, in shades of white, pink, or purplish red. Oval, 4 to 6-inch leaves unfold after the flowers fade. *M. soulangiana*'s varieties stay under 10 feet in all but the largest containers.

The star magnolia (*M. stellata*) grows slowly to 10 feet tall. Its star-shaped spring blooms are white to rosy pink, up to 5 inches across.

You can plant magnolias at almost any time of year—but if you purchase them in spring, you can see the flower shape and color. Follow the planting guidelines on pages 96 to 97, using a large or extra-large container (see page 84). Fill container with a lightweight potting soil mix; keep soil moist, but not soggy. From spring through summer, apply a complete fertilizer monthly (apply timed-release fertilizer less often, following package directions). Place in full sun, protected from extreme heat and wind.

Nerium oleander (oleander)

Mahonia
Oregon grape

Oregon grape is a showy shrub with an interesting vertical branch structure and glossy, spiny-tipped leaves. Clusters of yellow flowers blossom in early spring, followed by blue summertime berries with a powdery bloom. The berries are edible and make a tasty jelly. Oregon grape grows from 2 to 8 feet tall in a container; it tolerates most climates.

Plant this shrub at almost any time of year, following the guidelines on pages 96 to 97. Use a medium to large container (see page 84) filled with a lightweight potting soil mix. Keep soil moist, but not soggy. From spring through summer, apply a complete fertilizer once a month (apply timed-release fertilizer less often, following package directions). To keep foliage deep green, place shrub in a spot that receives afternoon shade.

Nandina domestica
Heavenly bamboo

Though *Nandina* resembles bamboo (*Bambusa*, page 54), the two plant groups are actually unrelated. This showy shrub offers white flowers in spring or summer and red berries in autumn and winter. The fine-textured foliage, borne on striking canelike stems, turns crimson in winter. Heavenly bamboo is a good selection if you're hunting for a delicate-looking, upright-growing container subject (mature plants reach 5 to 8 feet). *N. d.* 'Nana', a smaller type, grows only about 1 foot tall.

Plant heavenly bamboo in a large container (see page 84) at almost any time of year, following the guidelines on pages 96 to 97. Use a lightweight potting soil mix; keep soil moist, but not soggy. From spring through summer, apply a

complete fertilizer once a month (apply timed-release fertilizer less often, following package directions). Place in full sun or partial shade.

Nerium oleander
Oleander

Pictured at left and on page 6

Tough and easy to grow, oleander also puts on a colorful and long-lasting show of flowers: large clusters of white, pink, peach, yellow, or red single or double blossoms appear from May or June through October. One warning about this otherwise "perfect" shrub—all parts of the plant are poisonous if eaten. Caution children against eating leaves or flowers, and don't burn branches—the smoke can cause severe irritation.

Oleander is a quick-growing shrub that can reach 12 feet when mature, though with pruning (see pages 104 to 106) you can hold it to moderate size for years. A row of oleanders planted in large containers makes an excellent screen. Dwarf oleanders such as *Nerium oleander* 'Petite Pink' and *N. o.* 'Petite Salmon' are easily kept to 3 or 4 feet. *N. o.* 'Algiers' (single dark red) and *N. o.* 'Casablanca' (single pure white) are intermediate size.

Oleander tolerates hot weather well, so it does better than most evergreen shrubs in desert and hot inland areas. (It also tolerates soil with a relatively high salt content.) Where winters are frosty, oleander needs overhead protection (under an eave, for example) during winter.

Plant oleander at almost any time of year, following the guidelines on pages 96 to 97. Use a large or extra-large container (see page 84) filled with a mix of half lightweight potting soil mix, half garden loam. Allow soil to dry out somewhat between waterings. From spring through summer, apply a complete fertilizer once a month (apply timed-release fertilizer less often, following package directions). A full-sun location suits oleander best.

Phormium
New Zealand flax

Container-grown New Zealand flax can provide a dramatic accent on a deck or patio—it may reach 6 feet or more, sending up numerous stiff, swordlike leaves arranged in a fan pattern. Dusky red and yellow flowers cluster atop stems standing high above the leaves. Varieties are available with leaves of bronze, red, purple, and green striped with creamy white. *Phormium* 'Tiny Tim' grows 3 to 4 feet tall, has bronzy leaves striped yellow.

You can plant flax at almost any time of year. Use a large container (see page 84), and follow the general planting guidelines on pages 96 to 97. Flax tolerates almost any type of soil, but it does best in a mix of half lightweight potting soil mix, half garden loam. Allow soil to dry out somewhat between waterings. Every 2 months, from spring through autumn, apply a complete fertilizer. (Apply timed-release fertilizer less often, following package directions.) Give full sun or partial shade.

Where winters are severe, protect plant by wrapping it in burlap or placing it in an unheated greenhouse, basement, or garage.

Pieris japonica
Flame-of-the-forest, lily-of-the-valley shrub, pieris

This relative of *Rhododendron* (facing page) looks attractive the year around. Flower buds resembling strings of tiny pinkish or dark red beads appear in early winter; in late winter or early spring, they open to clusters of white, pink, or nearly red blossoms. Shortly after the plant blooms, young leaves unfurl on the tiered branches—bronzy red at first, green and leathery later on. Most pieris grow upright to about 8 feet, but lower-growing varieties such as *Pieris japonica* 'Valley Rose' (with pink-tinged leaves) and *P. j.* 'Crispa' (with wavy-edged leaves) are available. *P. j.* 'Variegata' grows very slowly. Its leaves, marked with creamy white, are pink-tinged in spring.

You can plant this shrub at almost any time of year. Follow the guidelines on pages 96 to 97, using a large container (see page 84) filled with an acid soil mix (see page 95). Keep soil moist, but not soggy. From spring through summer, apply an acid fertilizer (see page 102) monthly. (Apply timed-release fertilizer less often, following package directions.) Give pieris full sun in cool, humid climates, partial shade elsewhere.

Pittosporum (pittosporum)

Pittosporum
Golden fragrance, pittosporum, tobira, Victorian box

Pictured below left and on page 9

Pittosporum varies in form—some types are low (1 to 2 feet tall) and compact, others as tall as trees (12 feet or more). But all kinds are dependable evergreen container shrubs. Though some types have flowers or decorative fruit, most are valued primarily for their thick, handsome foliage. In some, the foliage is pleasantly fragrant: *Pittosporum eugenioides*, *P. napaulense* (golden fragrance), *P. tobira* (tobira), *P. undulatum* (Victorian box), and *P. viridiflorum* (Cape pittosporum). Trim shrubs into formal shapes, if you wish; or use taller plants to create a natural screen.

Plant at almost any time of year, following the guidelines on pages 96 to 97; use a large container (see page 84) filled with a mix of half lightweight potting soil mix, half garden loam. Allow soil to dry out somewhat between waterings. From spring through summer, apply a complete fertilizer monthly (apply timed-release fertilizer less often, following package directions). All types perform best in full or half-day sun. Pittosporum is susceptible to attack by aphids and scale insects; see page 109 for controls.

Podocarpus
Fern pine, yew pine

Pictured on page 30

If you're looking for a suitable espalier subject (see page 105), here it is. The limber branches of this small, tidy tree take gracefully to training, though you can let them drape naturally if you prefer. The fern pine (*Podocarpus gracilior*) has grayish green leaves; leaves of the yew pine (*P. macrophyllus*) are bright green and broader than those of *P. gracilior*. Both types are reliable, slow-growing shrubs that remain vigorous for many years in the same pot.

You can plant *Podocarpus* at almost any time of year. Follow the guidelines on pages 96 to 97, using a large container (see page 84) filled with a mix of half lightweight potting soil mix, half garden loam. Keep soil moist, but not soggy. From spring through summer, apply a complete fertilizer once a month (apply timed-release fertilizer less often, following package directions). Give *Podocarpus* full sun or partial shade.

Prunus laurocerasus
English laurel

Pictured on page 12

A traditional favorite for geometric shaping (but good-looking even without such shaping), English laurel can reach 6 to 8 feet in a container. It's fast-growing, evergreen, and dense, with glossy dark green leaves from 3 to 7 inches long.

At almost any time of year, plant English laurel in a large or extra-large container (see page 84) filled with a mix of half lightweight potting soil mix, half garden loam. Follow the planting guidelines on pages 96 to 97. Keep soil moist, but not soggy; from spring through summer, apply a complete fertilizer once a month (apply timed-release fertilizer less often, following package directions). Give this shrub partial shade where summers get hot; elsewhere, it prefers full sun.

Pyracantha
Firethorn, pyracantha

This shrub grows in an irregular, informal shape. Though a few newer pyracantha hybrids are thornless, most varieties have sharp thorns; these prickly specimens make good barrier plantings. Taller types (reaching 6 to 10 feet) take nicely to espaliering (see page 105). Dwarf kinds are naturals for containers. From summer through autumn, pyracantha bears bright scarlet berries that birds consider very tasty.

At almost any time of year, plant pyracantha in a large container (see page 84), following the general guidelines on pages 96 to 97. Use a mix of half lightweight potting soil mix, half garden loam. Let soil dry out somewhat between waterings. From spring through summer, apply a complete fertilizer once a month (apply timed-release fertilizer less often, following package directions). Place shrub in a full-sun location.

Raphiolepis indica
India hawthorn

Pictured on page 9

India hawthorn is a good-looking, compact shrub, well known for its willingness to grow in a variety of conditions. The pointed, leathery leaves are bronzy red when young, deep green when mature; clusters of pink blossoms, borne from winter through spring, combine well with rhododendrons, bulbs, and other spring flowers. After the blossoms fade, the glossy foliage provides an attractive backdrop for summer and autumn-blooming flowers.

Though some varieties of India hawthorn reach 7 feet, most types grow 4 feet tall at the most. This shrub is a good choice for a container standard (tree form—see page 106).

You can plant India hawthorn at almost any time of year. Follow the general guidelines on pages 96 to 97, using a medium to large container (see page 84). Fill container with a lightweight potting soil mix (some gardeners mix in garden loam, half and half). Let soil dry out somewhat between waterings. From spring through summer, apply a complete fertilizer once a month (apply timed-release fertilizer less often, following package directions). Give it full sun.

Rhododendron
Azalea, rhododendron

Pictured below right and on pages 9, 16, 17, 18, 19, 27

Unless you live in a region where winter temperatures dip below $-15°F/-26°C$, you can probably grow some kind of azalea or rhododendron in an outdoor container. When well tended, these shrubs offer a springtime floral extravaganza, producing abundant blooms in creamy white and every possible shade of red, purple, pink, and yellow. And thanks to their elegant dark green foliage, they look attractive even after the blooming season is over.

There are about a dozen different groups of azaleas (both evergreen and deciduous) to choose from; Belgian Indica, Southern Indica, and Kurume types are especially good selections. The Satsuki type makes a wonderful hanging basket plant.

Container-grown rhododendrons may reach 4 to 6 feet. Azaleas are smaller; depending on the variety, they grow from 1 to 3 feet tall.

You can plant these shrubs at almost any time of year, but it's probably best to buy during the spring blooming season, when you can choose just the flower shape, size, and color you prefer. Follow the planting guidelines on pages 96 to 97. Use a 12 to 14-inch pot for a gallon-can-size azalea; for rhododendrons (usually sold in 5-gallon cans), large or extra-large containers (see page 84) are best. Fill containers with an acid soil mix (see page 95); keep soil moist, but not soggy. When the blooming season ends, begin applications of an acid fertilizer (choose one that's specially formulated for azaleas and rhododendrons), following label directions carefully for timing and amount.

These plants need a spot that's shaded from hot afternoon sun and protected from wind. During extremely cold weather, provide overhead protection to prevent damage from frost and wind (under an eave, for example—see page 103).

Rosa
Rose

Pictured on page 62

No other flowering shrub is quite so famous, beloved, or widely planted as the rose. For its beauty as well as its ruggedness and versatility, this plant has long been a favorite among container gardeners.

As a rule, the polyanthas, floribundas, and miniatures take best to containers. These are bushy, compact types that attain only moderate height—and they flower from spring right through summer. Grandifloras and hybrid teas perform less well; almost all are deep-rooted, bulky plants that don't adapt easily to a confined space. If you long to try a hybrid tea in a container, choose a shorter or thin-caned type.

For a miniature rose, use a small container (see page 84). For the larger types, though, it's best to avoid containers with tapered sides; these usually don't provide enough room for the plant's roots. Instead, use straight-sided wooden boxes, square or rectangular. (Half barrels are another good choice.) Boxes for polyanthas and smaller floribundas should be at least 14 inches square; short hybrid teas and taller-growing floribundas need 16 to 20-inch boxes. Whatever size box you use, make sure it's at least 16 inches deep.

Plant roses at almost any time of year, following the general guidelines on pages 96 to 97. You can buy bushes in nursery cans the year around; bareroot roses are available in winter and early spring. Use a mix of half garden loam, half lightweight potting soil mix, and add a handful (about a 4-inch potful) of bonemeal to the soil of each container—about a teaspoon of bonemeal to a miniature rose's container.

Water roses sparingly until growth begins in spring, allowing soil to dry out somewhat between waterings. After growth starts, keep soil moist, but not soggy. Apply a complete fertilizer just as growth begins in spring, again after the main blooming period, and once more when the plant begins to put out growth for an autumn crop of flowers. Locate roses in full or half-day sun where air circulation is good.

Roses are subject to leaf spot, powdery mildew, and rust (see page 108); also watch for aphids, spider mites, and thrips (see page 109).

Rhododendron (azalea)

For fragrance fanciers

Most of the time, we think of beauty as something seen, something that "lies in the eyes of the beholder." But one whiff of a rose proves immediately that a different sort of beauty delights the sense of smell. In fact, certain fragrant plants have long been prized just as much as those with lovely looks or tasty fruits. The wafted scent may be heady and rich enough to detect from several yards away—or so delicate that you have to lean over to sniff at close range.

If fragrance is your fancy, you can savor a considerable sampling of it, even with just a small container collection. All the plants listed below will transform the air around them in a deliciously scented way; many are traditional choices for cut flowers, as well.

A scented plant's fragrance may reside in its flowers, its foliage, or both; in our list, we note which part of each plant is fragrant. Floral perfume tends to smell strongest in warm, humid weather, fainter on days that are hot and dry. From foliage, you'll get the sharpest whiff in any weather by touching the leaves.

Though most of our listed plants are appealing to the human nose, they don't seem to attract birds and bees—or at least, no more so than other plants. (Four of the suggested plants—citrus, lavender, rosemary, and wisteria—do attract bees.)

Miniature tree rose, 'Bojangles', is at perfect height for sniffing.

	Fragrant flowers	Fragrant foliage	See page no.
ANNUALS, PERENNIALS, BULBS			
Freesia (freesia)	X		48
Hyacinthus (hyacinth)	X		49
Lathyrus odoratus (sweet pea)	X		34
Lavandula angustifolia (English lavender)	X	X	42
Lilium (lily)	X		49
Matthiola incana (stock)	X		35
Narcissus (narcissus)	X		50
Pelargonium (scented geranium)		X	43
VINES			
Trachelospermum jasminoides (star jasmine)	X		53
Wisteria (wisteria)	X		53
SHRUBS			
Daphne odora (winter daphne)	X		56
Gardenia (gardenia)	X		58
Juniperus (juniper)		X	58
Rosa (rose)	X		61
Rosemary		X	78
TREES			
Citrus (kumquat, lemon, lime, orange, tangelo)	X		80
Malus (flowering crabapple)	X		65
Prunus blireiana (flowering plum)	X		66

Trees

Tall Italian cypress or willowy weeping birch, lacy Japanese maple or fragrant sweet bay—trees bring natural grace wherever they grow. Container-cultivated trees—modest in height, yet still tall enough to look dramatic—can enhance even the smallest entryway, patio, or balcony.

Decked out in green the year around, conifers and other evergreens create a lush background for blooming annuals and perennials. Some come indoors as Christmas trees, too (see page 67).

Install stake when pot is half filled with soil.

Many deciduous trees stage seasonal spectacles worth showing off to friends. Blazing with color in autumn and elegantly bare-branched in winter, they burst into bloom in spring, then spend the summer in lavish leaf. And trees bring more than good looks to their surroundings: they help to shelter the places where they grow.

With proper care, most slow-growing small trees will prosper in large containers for years; consult page 84 to make sure you choose a tub, barrel, or planter box that's large enough for your tree. Any container—no matter how ample—slows a tree's growth and limits the height it can achieve: a specimen that might reach 30 feet growing in the open ground may attain only 8 to 10 feet in its tub. You can also keep height and width in check by pruning (see pages 104 to 106).

You can plant trees whenever you choose, but early autumn is best in mild-winter climates, spring in cold-winter areas. Most trees perform best in a mix of one part garden loam to two parts lightweight potting soil mix. Keep soil slightly on the dry side (water deeply, then allow soil to dry out); apply a complete fertilizer once in spring, once again in summer.

During its first years, even a small tree may be top-heavy and thus subject to wind damage. Give a young tree a supporting stake at planting time (see drawing above); tie the tree loosely to the stake with one of the elastic or padded ties available at nurseries.

Abies
Fir

Nordmann fir (*Abies nordman-niana*), noble fir (*A. procera*), and white fir (*A. concolor*)—three very handsome trees—adapt comfortably to containers. Nordmann fir wears a dense coat of dark green needles. Noble fir has short stiff branches covered with bluish green needles; white fir's 2-inch needles are also bluish green. These species accept warmer climates than most firs do; you can even bring them indoors for Christmas (see page 67). They grow slowly, but will eventually attain a height of 20 feet or more if not pruned (see pages 104 to 106).

Plant any of these firs at almost any time of year, following the guidelines on pages 96 to 97. Give each tree a large or extra-large container (see page 84) filled with a mix of one-third garden loam, two-thirds lightweight potting soil mix. Allow soil to dry out somewhat between waterings. Apply a complete fertilizer once in spring, once again in summer. Place in full sun.

Acer palmatum
Japanese maple

Pictured below and on pages 14, 17, 29

This lacy-looking tree changes color with the seasons. Leaves are pink, red, or pale green tinted with red when they emerge in spring; they turn green in summer, then yellow, orange, pink, or bright scarlet in autumn. Delicate bare branches are lovely to look at in winter. Good low-growing varieties for containers are 'Dissectum', 'Crimson Queen', and 'Ever Red'. Japanese maple grows 6 to 15 feet tall unless pruned (see pages 104 to 105).

Plant in early autumn or spring, following the guidelines on pages 96 to 97. A 5-gallon-size Japanese maple does well in a 16 to 18-inch tub. As it grows, give it an extra-large container (see page 84) filled with a mix of one-third garden loam, two-thirds lightweight potting soil mix. Keep soil moist, but not soggy. Apply a complete fertilizer once in spring, once again in summer. Place tree in a location that receives morning sun and afternoon shade; protect from reflected heat and drying winds.

Acer palmatum (Japanese maple) and *Impatiens wallerana* (busy Lizzie, impatiens)

Araucaria
Bunya-bunya, Norfolk Island pine, star pine

Pictured below right

Araucaria heterophylla is an excellent container tree, healthy and happy whether growing indoors or out. Its horizontal tiers of feathery growth give it the look of a pine tree—but despite its appearance and its common names (Norfolk Island pine and star pine), this tree isn't a true pine.

Leaves of the bunya-bunya (*A. bidwillii*) grow in overlapping spirals along its branches. Both bunya-bunya and Norfolk Island pine grow slowly to a great height (100 feet) in the garden, but rarely exceed 12 feet in a container.

Plant either *Araucaria* at almost any time of year, following the guidelines on pages 96 to 97. Use a large container (see page 84) filled with a lightweight potting soil mix. Keep soil moist, but not soggy; apply a complete fertilizer once in spring, once again in summer. (Apply timed-release fertilizer less often, following package directions.) A full-sun location is best, though these trees can also tolerate partial shade.

Bring inside for winter in all but the mildest climates, placing trees in a cool spot receiving bright reflected light. (Norfolk Island pine makes a lovely living Christmas tree—see page 67.)

Arbutus unedo
Strawberry tree

This cheery-looking evergreen tree has dark green, red-stemmed leaves. Its round, nubbly fruits turn from green to yellow to red as they ripen, usually reaching maturity just as drooping clusters of white flowers open in late autumn or winter. (Fruit looks much better than it tastes—it's mealy and flavorless.)

Variety 'Compacta', a dwarf strawberry tree, is a striking container plant that makes a beautiful accent in a small entry garden. Even after 10 years, it will be only 4 to 5 feet tall. Variety 'Elfin King' is even smaller. (Standard-size trees grow from 8 to 35 feet.)

Plant dwarf or standard-size strawberry trees at almost any time of year, one to a large or extra-large container (see page 84) filled with a lightweight potting soil mix. Follow the planting guidelines on pages 96 to 97. Allow soil to dry out somewhat between waterings; apply a complete fertilizer once in spring, once again in summer. (Apply timed-release fertilizer less often, following package directions.) Strawberry tree likes a full-sun location.

Betula pendula
European white birch, weeping birch

A perennially popular landscape tree, European white birch also looks attractive in a container. It's particularly beautiful in autumn, when its leaves turn a bright golden yellow. You can plant two or three birches in a single extra-large container to achieve the look of a small grove, or line up several trees in individual containers to make a lacy but effective garden screen.

European white birch usually grows from 30 to 40 feet tall, but it's likely to reach only half that height when grown in a container.

Plant at almost any time of year, following the guidelines on pages 96 to 97. Use a large or extra-large container (see page 84) filled with a mix of one-third garden loam, two-thirds lightweight soil mix. Allow soil to dry out somewhat between waterings. From spring through summer, apply a complete fertilizer once in spring, once again in summer. Locate in full sun. Aphids may cause problems; see page 109 for control measures.

Callistemon citrinus
Lemon bottlebrush

A familiar landscape shrub, lemon bottlebrush also serves beautifully as a container tree. It's especially effective as a natural screen (depending upon variety and container size, it may reach 8 to 12 feet). Its 6-inch flowers look just like bright red bottle brushes; hummingbirds love them.

Plant at almost any time of year, following the guidelines on pages 96 to 97. Use a large or extra-large container (see page 84) filled with a mix of one-third garden loam, two-thirds lightweight potting soil mix. Let soil dry out somewhat between waterings. Apply a complete fertilizer once in spring, once again in summer. Give bottlebrush a full-sun location.

Cedrus deodara
Deodar cedar

Pictured on facing page and page 14

Only compact forms of this popular conifer thrive in containers for any length of time. Three such forms are available: *Cedrus deodara* 'Pendula', cascading in shape; *C. d.* 'Repandens', which has stiff horizontal branches; and *C. d.* 'Descanso Dwarf', which has sweeping limbs. These are eye-catching trees, best used as a focal point in the garden. You can prune these cedars (see pages 104 to 106) to hold them to 6 to 12 feet. To make trees more dense, cut new growth on side branches halfway back in late spring.

Plant at almost any time of year, following the guidelines on pages 96 to 97. Each tree needs a large or extra-large container (see page 84) filled with a lightweight potting soil mix. Let soil dry out somewhat between waterings; apply a complete fertilizer once in spring, once again in summer. All types of deodar cedar need a full-sun location.

Cercis canadensis
Eastern redbud

Early in spring, Eastern redbud's branches are covered with sweet-pea-shaped blossoms of deep, purplish pink. The blooming tree looks best when standing alone, since its vivid flowers may clash with the blossoms of other plants. (The white-flowered variety 'Alba' does blend beautifully with other spring flowers.) Redbuds can reach 12 to 16 feet in a container, but pruning (see pages 104 to 105) will keep them smaller.

Plant at almost any time of year, following the guidelines on pages 96 to 97; use a large container (see page 84) filled with a mix of one-third garden loam, two-thirds lightweight potting soil mix. Let soil dry out somewhat between waterings. Apply a complete fertilizer once in spring, once again in summer.

Eastern redbud needs full, bright sun for best growth.

Araucaria heterophylla
(Norfolk Island pine)

Cupressus sempervirens
Italian cypress

Standing straight and tall as a sentinel, Italian cypress provides a strong vertical accent that few trees can match. Its tiny, scalelike leaves are usually bright green, but there's one named variety—'Glauca'—with blue green foliage. (Two other popular varieties, 'Indica' and 'Stricta', have bright green leaves.) Pruning (see pages 104 to 106) will keep a container plant to 10 feet or so. Topping to control height can result in increased growth of side branches.

Plant at almost any time of year, using a large or extra-large container (see page 94) filled with a mix of one-third garden loam, two-thirds lightweight potting soil mix. Follow the guidelines on pages 96 to 97. Allow soil to dry out somewhat between waterings. Apply a complete fertilizer once in spring, once again in summer. Locate in full sun. Spider mites may be a problem; see page 109 for methods of control.

Fagus sylvatica
European beech

Pictured below

Its sleek gray bark and glossy leaves make the deciduous European beech an eye-catching container subject. Tricolor beech (*Fagus sylvatica* 'Tricolor') has green leaves edged in white and pink; weeping copper beech (*F. s.* 'Purpurea Pendula') has purple leaves. A third good container choice is *F. s.* 'Zlatia', the golden beech. Its leaves are yellow when young, yellow green when mature. Pruning will keep to 10 to 20 feet tall, half their height in the ground (see pages 104 to 105).

Beeches thrive in large or extra-large containers (see page 84) filled with a mix of one-third garden loam, two-thirds lightweight potting soil mix. Plant them at almost any time of year, following the guidelines on pages 96 to 97. Allow soil to dry out somewhat between waterings; apply a complete fertilizer once in spring, once again in summer. Place in full sun or partial shade.

Laurus nobilis
Grecian laurel, sweet bay

This formal-looking evergreen tree bears the aromatic leaf used in cooking. Often pruned into topiary— spheres, cones, and pillars—bays are classic container trees, long valued for their hardiness and dependability. Clusters of creamy yellow flowers bloom in spring or summer, followed by small purple to black berries; both flowers and fruit are inconspicuous.

Sweet bay grows slowly, eventually reaching 12 feet in a container; keep it smaller by pruning as described on pages 104 to 106.

Plant sweet bay almost any time of year, following the guidelines on pages 96 to 97. Use a large or extra-large container (see page 84) filled with a lightweight potting soil mix. Allow soil to dry out somewhat between waterings. Apply a complete fertilizer once in spring, once again in summer. Locate in full sun or partial shade.

Malus
Flowering crabapple

To grow this lavishly flowering tree in a container, select a small, slow-growing variety such as 'Almey', 'Pink Spire', or 'Purple Wave'; flower color choices include white, pink, and deep rose. Small fruits, appealing to birds, appear in autumn.

Flowering crabapple will eventually reach a height of 6 to 12 feet. Annual pruning isn't necessary.

Plant at almost any time of year, following the guidelines on pages 96 to 97; use a large or extra-large container (see page 84) filled with a mix of one-third garden loam, two-thirds lightweight potting soil mix. Let soil dry out somewhat between waterings. Apply a complete fertilizer once in spring, once again in summer. Locate in full sun.

Flowering crabapple is subject to fireblight disease, so it's wise to purchase a resistant type. For other pests and diseases, see entry for dwarf apple trees on page 80.

Fagus sylvatica (European beech)

Cedrus deodara (deodar cedar)

Picea
Spruce

Pictured below and on facing page

Long-time favorites for container gardens, these lovely evergreens are excellent candidates for living Christmas trees (see facing page). Popular choices include Norway spruce (*Picea abies*) and Colorado blue spruce (*P. pungens* 'Glauca'). Dwarf varieties are good selections, too; one example is *P. glauca* 'Conica', dwarf Alberta spruce (also called dwarf white spruce). Covered in soft grayish green needles, this little tree grows very slowly to 7 feet.

You can plant spruces at almost any time of year. Following the planting guidelines on pages 96 to 97, set each tree in a large or extra-large container (see page 84) filled with a mix of one-third garden loam, two-thirds lightweight potting soil mix. Let soil dry out somewhat between waterings; apply a complete fertilizer once in spring, once again in summer. Spruce trees like full sun, but they need protection from reflected heat and drying winds.

Pinus
Pine

Pictured on pages 14 and 28

The pine group includes hundreds of members; several of these prosper in large tubs or half barrels.

Bristlecone pine (*Pinus aristata*), bushy and dense, has branches that sweep the ground. It grows slowly to 20 feet, but looks attractive pruned to smaller size.

Shore pine (*P. contorta*), densely decked out with foliage, grows symmetrically to a narrow crown. It can attain a height of 20 to 35 feet, but looks attractive pruned to any size.

Picea glauca 'Conica' (dwarf Alberta spruce)

The handsome Japanese red pine (*P. densiflora*) often forms two or more trunks. Keep it away from hot and dry winds, and cold gusts. If not pruned, it grows quite tall—over 20 feet.

Mugho pine (*P. mugo mugo*) is a dense-foliaged tree that has a very pleasing shape. It slowly reaches a height of just 4 feet. Be sure to protect this tree from desert dryness.

Japanese black pine (*P. thunbergiana*) has an irregular, spreading shape. It can reach 20 feet or more, but pruning (see pages 104 to 106) will keep it lower. This tree tolerates pruning well; it's a favorite choice for bonsai (page 54) and living Christmas trees.

Other pine trees that are especially suitable for living Christmas trees (see facing page) are *P. eldarica, P. halepensis, P. radiata,* and *P. sylvestris.*

With proper care, pines easily thrive for 10 years or more in a container. Plant at almost any time of year, following the general guidelines on pages 96 to 97. Each of the pines described above requires a large or extra-large container (see page 84) filled with a mix of one-third garden loam or compost, two-thirds lightweight potting soil mix. Allow soil to dry out somewhat between waterings. Apply a complete fertilizer once in spring, once again in summer. All pines need full sun to look their best.

Prunus
Flowering cherry, flowering plum

Breathtaking when arrayed in its pink-and-white spring blossoms, flowering cherry also looks attractive when not in bloom. Several species and many varieties are available; any one makes a dramatic entryway tree or brings elegance to a patio or deck.

Flowering plum (*Prunus blireiana*) offers fragrant, semidouble to double, bright pink springtime blossoms. Its leaves are reddish purple when they unfold in spring, turning to bronze in summer.

Both cherry and plum grow to about 20 feet; you can keep them smaller with judicious pruning (see pages 104 to 105). Cut branches while tree is in bloom and use branches in arrangements.

Plant either flowering cherry or flowering plum in early autumn or spring, following the general guidelines on pages 96 to 97. For each tree, use a large or extra-large container (see page 84) filled with a mix of one-third garden loam, two-thirds lightweight potting soil mix. Keep soil moist, but not soggy. Apply a complete fertilizer once in spring, once again in summer. Locate in full sun.

Sequoia sempervirens
Coast redwood

Probably the West Coast's most famous native tree, this fast-growing evergreen readily adapts to life in a container. You can make an instant natural screen (about 8 feet tall) with a row of 15-gallon-size redwoods planted in 28-inch boxes. Or use these trees to create a thick evergreen background for a deck.

Redwoods are famous for the immense height they can achieve in the ground, but containers will severely restrict their growth. Prune to keep them to the size you want (see pages 104 to 106). Some gardeners "top" them by cutting back the central trunk, producing a more horizontal tree.

Plant at almost any time of year, following the general guidelines on pages 96 to 97. Give each tree a large or extra-large container (see page 84) filled with a mix of one-third garden loam, two-thirds lightweight potting soil mix. Keep soil moist, but not soggy. Apply a complete fertilizer once in spring, once again in summer. Locate in full sun or partial shade.

Living Christmas trees

How can you be assured of a green, fresh Christmas tree every year? It's simple: grow your tree in a container. For most of the year, it's a lovely evergreen presence on deck or patio; at holiday time, it brings its special spicy-fragranced magic indoors.

If you're buying a tree just before Christmas, try to find one that has lived in its nursery container for a year or more. A tree only recently dug from a field has probably left some of its roots behind, and declined in vigor as a result. But regardless of how well established a tree is, it should spend no more than 7 to 10 days indoors.

The day before you bring your tree inside, soak it thoroughly; then move it to an indoor spot that's well away from the fireplace and other heat sources. Place the tree on a drip saucer (be sure to protect the floor under the saucer). Water with trayfuls of ice cubes every few days; the cubes melt slowly, providing a gentle, steady supply of moisture.

These 3 to 8-foot conifers in big tubs of soil may weigh 150 to 200 pounds, so expect to roll your tree inside on a hand truck (see page 93 for other ideas).

After you've enjoyed the tree inside for a week or so, return it outdoors. If it has spent over a year in its pot, you can safely set it almost anywhere, in full sun or partial shade. But if it's a fairly recent transplant, protect it from hot afternoon sun and drying winds.

Apply a complete fertilizer once in spring, once again in summer. For more information on general care of container trees, see page 63; for repotting advice, consult page 97.

Following is a list of favorite evergreen trees to grow outside most of the year, then bring indoors during the Christmas season.

Abies concolor
White fir

Somewhat compact, symmetrical fir with blue green 1 to 2-inch-long needles. Slightly more compact than Noble fir (below). See page 63.

Abies procera
Noble fir

More open that the Douglas fir but still pyramidal. Short, stiff branches, thickly covered in blue green, 1-inch-long needles. See page 63.

Araucaria heterophylla
Norfolk Island pine

Moderately fast-growing tree with evenly spaced "layers" of branches, fully coated with small medium green needles. An unusual but popular choice. See page 64.

Picea abies
Norway spruce

Fast-growing symmetrical spruce with a shape favored for Christmas trees. Stiff branches with deep green needles. See page 66.

Picea glauca 'Conica'
Dwarf Alberta spruce

Extremely compact pyramidal spruce; extremely slow growing (7 feet in 35 years). Short, soft, gray needles. See page 66.

Picea pungens
Colorado spruce

A Christmas classic with very stiff, horizontal branches forming a symmetrical pyramid. Needle color varies

Festive Colorado spruce (*Picea pungens*) comes into the living room (its saucer is sealed so water won't reach the carpet).

from dark green to blue green or steely blue. See page 66.

Pinus eldarica
Modell pine

Another fast-growing tree (2½ to 4 feet a year). Needs shearing to maintain symmetrical shape. Dark green, 5 to 6½-inch-long needles. See page 66.

Pinus halepensis
Aleppo pine

A fast-growing pine (2½ to 3 feet a year in favorable conditions). Needs shearing to keep its youthful, symmetrical shape. Light green, 2½ to 4-inch needles. See page 66.

Pinus radiata
Monterey pine

Fast growing (2½ to 4 feet a year). Needs shearing to keep symmetrical shape. Bright green needles 3 to 7 inches long. See page 66.

Pinus sylvestris
Scotch pine

Pyramid-shaped pine with densely spaced branches, covered with 1½ to 3-inch-long, blue green, stiff needles. Branches droop with age, giving tree an irregular and picturesque shape. See page 66.

Pinus thunbergiana
Japanese black pine

Not always symmetrical by nature, but easily sheared into any desired shape. Bright green, stiff needles, 3 to 4½ inches long. See page 66.

Pseudotsuga menziesii
Douglas fir

Classic Christmas tree shape when young. Dense, soft needles, dark green to blue green, 1 to 1½ inches long, radiate out in all directions from branches and twigs. Sweet fragrance when crushed.

Indoor-outdoor plants

Many plants commonly thought of as year-round house plants take kindly to a spring and summer vacation outside. In addition to encouraging substantial spurts of growth, an outdoor home during the warmer months helps keep these plants healthy and happy when they return inside. Their changing seasonal residence can be a plus for you, too—these are double-duty decorators, adding leafy cheer inside during winter, then beautifying porch or patio in warm weather.

Let plants adapt to outdoors in protected spot.

Here and on the following pages, we describe a few of the plants that do best with this type of dual environment. Beyond the fact that all enjoy an indoor-outdoor way of life, they're a diverse group, ranging from colorful coleus to easy-care philodendron.

Though outdoor light is always more intense than the light plants receive indoors, those that like shade or filtered sun—*Aspidistra elatior* (cast-iron plant) and all types of ferns, for example—can safely move directly from indoors to their outdoor vacation homes. But when you move a full-sun lover like hibiscus outside, proceed cautiously; the intensity of direct outdoor sun will come as a shock. Don't immediately set the plant in the sunniest portion of the patio—this could damage or even kill it. Instead, place it under an overhang for a week or two (see drawing above); then spend about 2 weeks gently easing it into the proper amount of sunlight. Start by placing it on the north side of the house. After a few days, move it to the east side, where it will catch the morning sun. In another week, the plant will be ready to take some direct afternoon sun. After 2 weeks, a sun-loving type will be ready to soak up bright light.

Also take care to water these plants attentively after you move them outside; their soil is likely to dry out faster than it did indoors. When you bring plants back inside, wash each plant with soapy water to remove pests, and withhold the first application of fertilizer until days become longer in early spring.

Aspidistra elatior
Cast-iron plant

As its common name implies, *Aspidistra elatior* is a rugged specimen that can take a great deal of abuse; it was popular in Victorian times, managing to stay alive in the typically dark, musty drawing rooms of that period. Its gracefully curved leaves are pointed at the tips; glossy and dark green, they grow up to 2 feet long and 4 inches wide. A full-grown plant forms a clump about 2 feet tall (and just as wide).

Grow cast-iron plant in almost any size container, depending on the size of the plant. Use a lightweight potting soil mix; keep soil moist, but not soggy. From spring through summer, apply a complete fertilizer once a month (apply timed-release fertilizer less often, following package directions). Outdoors, cast-iron plant prefers full or partial shade; it doesn't like direct sun.

In cold climates, bring the plant indoors during winter, placing it in a cool, low-light spot. (Where the weather stays temperate all year, cast-iron plant is happy to spend all its time outside.)

Coleus hybridus
Coleus, flame nettle, painted nettle

Pictured below

For a rich tapestry of subtle to brilliant colors, even in the shade, you can't beat coleus. Its oval, tooth-edged leaves, solid-colored or variegated, come in shades of brown, maroon, magenta, purple, red, orange, yellow, chartreuse, and green. Blue flower spikes are best pinched off (see page 104) in bud. When mature, coleus may reach a height of 2 feet or more.

Plant coleus seeds in spring, transplants at any time of year. Allow one plant to a 6 to 8-inch pot (thin seedlings accordingly). Use a lightweight potting soil mix, and keep soil moist, but not soggy. From spring through summer, apply a complete fertilizer at half the recommended monthly amount every 2 weeks (apply timed-release fertilizer less often, following package directions). Place containers in a filtered-sun location. Pinch growing tips regularly to encourage bushiness.

For winter-long splendor, move coleus indoors before the first autumn frost. It prefers average house temperatures and bright indirect light—even fluorescent light.

Coleus hybridus (coleus)

Ferns

Pictured below and on pages 7, 10, 13, 17, 21

Gardeners appreciate ferns for their fascinating foliage—from the delicate tracery of the maidenhair to the dramatic yet graceful fronds of tree types. You'll usually find several ferns in any house-plant fancier's collection—but these plants also add a striking accent outdoors, bring a lush, tropical or woodsy touch to patios, decks, balconies, and entryways. Ferns listed in the first group below happily spend spring and summer outdoors, but they must return inside for the cooler months. The second group—tree types—can stay outside all year in areas where winters are fairly mild. But in cold-winter regions, they too need protection from frost—either indoors, in a greenhouse, or under a patio roof or lanai.

Plant all ferns in a lightweight potting soil mix or an extra-lightweight mix (see page 95). Keep soil moist, but not soggy. Mist plants frequently, especially when they're spending time indoors, to help create the humid atmosphere they prefer. From spring through summer, apply a mild complete fertilizer (such as liquid fish emulsion) mixed at half the recommended monthly amount every 2 weeks. (Apply timed-release fertilizer less often, following package directions.) Outdoors, ferns prefer shade or filtered sun; while living inside, they like to sit where they'll receive plenty of bright light—but not direct sun. Average house temperatures suit them.

The following medium-size ferns (1 to 4 feet tall and just as wide) are just right for the medium-size containers described on page 84.

Adiantum—the group of maidenhair ferns—includes several types of fragile-looking ferns with bright green, finely cut fronds and wiry black stems. *Asparagus setaceus* (the popular asparagus fern), *A. densiflorus* 'Spengeri', and *A.d.* 'Meyers' are all related to edible asparagus; all have wiry stems and needlelike bright green leaflets. These lacy-looking ferns are lovely in hanging baskets (choose a dwarf variety of *A. setaceus*). *Asplenium nidus*, commonly called bird's nest fern, produces glossy, undivided apple green fronds with black ribs. *Davallia trichomanoides* looks best in a hanging basket. Its downward-curving, finely divided fronds may reach a length of 1 foot. This fern's common name—squirrel's foot fern—was inspired by the furry rhizomes that creep over the soil surface and down the sides of the pot holding the plant. Members of the group *Nephrolepis* (sword and Boston ferns) are deservedly popular for their feathery fronds and symmetri-cal appearance. Appearance varies slightly among the many named varieties of this group of ferns.

The large and dramatic tree ferns described below do well in a medium to large container (see page 84).

The Hawaiian tree fern (*Cibotium glaucum*) produces feathery, golden green fronds. It can attain an impressive size—6 feet tall and 8 feet wide. Slow-growing *Dicksonia antarctica,* the Tasmanian tree fern, is the most frost tolerant of tree types. Dark green, arching fronds, extending as far as 6 feet, grow from its fuzzy reddish brown trunk. *Sphaeropteris cooperi,* usually called Australian tree fern, is a fast-growing plant. It displays finely cut bright green fronds; broad and arching, they often extend to 10 feet.

Ficus
Indian laurel fig, rubber plant, weeping Chinese banyan

The genus *Ficus* includes not only the edible fig (*Ficus carica*), but a number of ornamental types that enjoy an indoor-outdoor life. The three described below are attractive evergreen trees.

The graceful weeping Chinese banyan (*Ficus benjamina*) has green, shiny 3 to 5-inch-long leaves. A container-grown tree can reach a height of 12 to 17 feet; if you don't want it to grow that tall, plant it in a medium-size container (see page 84).

The rubber plant, *F. elastica,* grows 3 to 10 feet tall. Its thick, glossy dark green leaves are 8 to 12 inches long.

Indian laurel fig (*F. microcarpa nitida*) has dense-foliaged, upward-stretching branches. It can reach 25 to 30 feet, but readily accepts repeated shearing to keep to a more modest height.

All three of the species above grow best in medium or large containers (see page 84). Use a lightweight potting soil mix or an extra-lightweight mix (see page 95). Let soil dry out somewhat between waterings. From spring through summer, apply a complete fertilizer monthly (apply timed-release fertilizer less often, following package directions). These trees do best in a spot where they'll receive morning sun only.

All ornamental figs are sensitive to cold, so bring them inside at the first sign of chilly weather. Indoors, they like average room temperatures and plenty of bright indirect light.

Though they ultimately benefit from a season or two spent out of doors, some *Ficus* (especially *F. benjamina*) may drop their leaves as a result of moving shock when you carry them outside in spring (or back indoors in autumn). If this happens to your tree, cut back on water, letting soil dry out almost completely between waterings. Growth should resume within 3 to 4 weeks; when it does, begin normal watering.

Hibiscus rosa-sinensis
Chinese hibiscus

One of the showiest of all flowering shrubs, Chinese hibiscus bursts into abundant bloom in summer, producing 4 to 6-inch blossoms in white or shades of pink, red, orange, or yellow. Though this glossy-foliaged shrub reaches impressive heights in its native tropics, it seldom exceeds 6 feet in a container.

Plant Chinese hibiscus in a medium-size container (see page 84) filled with a lightweight potting soil mix. Keep soil moist, but not soggy. From spring through summer, apply a complete fertilizer once a month (apply timed-release fertilizer less often, following package directions). Place in full sun.

At the first drop in autumn temperatures, move hibiscus indoors to a cool spot receiving lots of bright indirect light.

Davallia trichomanoides (squirrel's foot fern)

Cymbidium orchids

Among the easiest orchids to grow, cymbidiums bloom from February to early May, producing arching spikes of long-lasting flowers in white, pink, yellow, green, or bronze. Miniatures grow about 1½ feet tall with a slightly wider spread; standards reach up to four times that size.

Cymbidiums flower best if somewhat potbound. Plant them one to a medium-size container (see page 84). Use packaged orchid potting soil, or make your own by combining 2 parts fine redwood bark or sawdust, 2 parts peat moss, and 1 part river or quarry sand. Keep soil moist while new growth is developing (usually March through September); the rest of the year, allow soil to dry out almost completely. Apply a complete high-nitrogen liquid fertilizer (such as 15-15-15) every 10 days to 2 weeks, January to July. Make monthly applications of a low-nitrogen fertilizer (such as 5-10-10) August through December.

Where winter temperatures drop below 28°F./−2.2°C. for short periods, you can grow cymbidiums outdoors in partial sun all year, bringing them indoors while in bloom. In cold-winter areas, winter them indoors in bright filtered or indirect light.

Palms

Pictured at right

When a palm stands in a pot, its long, graceful fronds look doubly dramatic. Young plants do better indoors, but more mature ones will tolerate a protected outdoor site during warm weather.

Parlor palm (*Chamaedorea elegans*—widely sold as *Neanthe bella*) tolerates potbound conditions. It's just 3 to 4 feet tall when fully ma-

ture. For a lush look, group three or four plants in one large container.

Chamaedorea seifrizii, a palm with clustered trunks and dense growth, reaches 10 feet. Its feathery leaves divide into narrow leaflets.

The sentry or kentia palm, *Howea belmoreana*, tolerates dry soil. Its arching, feathery fronds are 6 to 7 feet long.

Lady palm (*Rhapis excelsa*) and rattan palm (*R. humilis*) produce bamboolike clumps of shiny, usually deep green foliage. These palms grow slowly to 12 feet and 18 feet, respectively.

Plant any of these palms in a medium to large container (see page 84) filled with a lightweight potting soil mix. Keep soil moist, but not soggy. From spring through autumn, apply a complete fertilizer once a month (apply timed-release fertilizer less often, following package directions). Indoors, these palms tolerate fairly low light levels and average house temperatures; outdoors, they need a warm partial-shade location that's protected from wind. When plants are outdoors, hose down fronds to minimize spider mite problems (see page 109).

Philodendron
Philodendron

This tough, durable plant is valued for its handsome, leathery leaves—heart shaped, deeply lobed, or arrow shaped. Upright forms (to 6 feet or more) and vining types are available; vining philodendrons usually require some kind of support.

Plant philodendron in a medium to large container (see page 84). Use a lightweight potting soil mix, and keep it moist, but not soggy. From spring through autumn, apply a complete fertilizer once a month (apply timed-release fertilizer less often, following package directions). Outdoors, philodendron likes a location sheltered from wind and hot, direct sun.

Bring the plant inside when weather cools off in autumn; give it average to warm house temperatures and bright indirect light.

Solanum pseudocapsicum
Jerusalem cherry

Bright red wintertime fruit follows Jerusalem cherry's summer show of white flowers. Though they resemble cherry tomatoes, *these fruits may be poisonous*—so when plants are bearing fruit, keep them out of reach of children. During the holiday season, dwarf forms of Jerusalem cherry (to 1 foot tall) are often sold for festive indoor decoration. Standard-size plants (3 to 4 feet tall) are also available, but they're not really suitable for containers.

Plant Jerusalem cherry in a small to medium container (see page 84) filled with a lightweight potting soil mix. Keep soil moist, but not soggy. From spring through summer, apply a complete fertilizer monthly (apply timed-release fertilizer less often, following package directions).

While in the house, Jerusalem cherry likes bright light (including some direct sun) and average room temperatures. You can move the plant outdoors to a full-sun location when all danger of frost is past. Pinch or lightly prune back its stems (see pages 104 to 105); new growth should appear within a week or so.

Chamaedorea elegans (parlor palm)

Cactuses & succulents, container attractions

Lemon yellow blossoms cover *Aeonium floribundum* in summer.

Cactuses and succulents are appealing, dramatic plants, best shown off in containers. Collecting them can be addictive—many a sizable garden has been inspired by the purchase of just one whimsical-looking specimen. (For detailed information, see *Sunset's Cactus and Succulents.*)

With rare exceptions, every cactus is a succulent—but not every succulent is a cactus. Cactuses are distinguished from other succulents by *areoles*—well-defined areas on the plant's surface from which sprout tufts of spines, bristles, or hairs. Cactus flowers always bloom from the areoles, too.

Planting tips. You can buy a special soil mix for cactuses and succulents at nurseries and garden centers. Or make your own: just combine one part leaf mold, one part peat-moss-based soil mix (the typical houseplant mix sold at nurseries is fine), and two parts river or quarry sand (not beach sand) or fine gravel.

Cactuses and succulents will thrive in almost any kind of pot. (If you use plastic pots, be very careful not to overwater.) For rounded plants, choose a container 2 inches wider in diameter than the plant; for more vertical plants, the pot diameter should be half the plant's height.

When you're planting spiny cactuses, you'll need to protect your hands. Wear gloves, and lift the cactus with a thick strap fashioned from folded newspaper.

Plant care. Cactuses and succulents are relatively easy to grow. Water them regularly during their active growth period (usually spring through summer); it's best to soak soil thoroughly each time you water, then let it dry out almost completely before the next watering. Also fertilize monthly during the growing season, using a complete liquid fertilizer (see page 102) diluted to one-quarter to one-half the recommended amount.

Stop fertilizing when plants enter their natural rest period (late autumn through winter); cut back on water, too, giving just enough to keep soil from drying out completely.

Cactuses and succulents need to soak up as much direct sunlight as possible for optimum health.

In all climates, these plants can sit safely indoors through the winter; where winters are cold, such shelter is essential. Give them the sunniest window in the house, and be sure to rotate pots a quarter turn every week to foster even growth.

Once a year, check to see if you need to repot; most cactuses and succulents require a new pot every 2 to 3 years. It's best to repot in early spring, just prior to the active growth season. If you see roots poking from the drainage hole or offsets (small new plants) crowding the parent plant, it's time for a move. See page 97 for repotting pointers.

Favorite plants. Below, we list some favorite cactuses and succulents for containers.

Aeonium

Group of decorative, shrubby plants, 6 to 36 inches tall; woody stems are crowned by rosettes of fleshy leaves. Flowers white, pink, or yellow.

Agave attenuata

An imposing container plant, 3 to 8 feet tall, with 2-foot-long spineless leaves. Trunk bears yellow green flowers on arching stems. Needs protection from frost and hottest sun.

Aloe

Main flower show runs from February to September. Clusters of red, orange, or yellow blooms are borne on spikes sprouting from clumps of fleshy, pointed leaves. Plant size varies from 6 inches to 10 feet.

Crassula argentea
Jade plant

Jade plant stays compact in a small container, but given a larger container, it may grow up to 6 feet tall. Small, pink star-shaped flowers bloom from November through April. (Photo on page 5.)

Echeveria
Hen and chicks

Attractive, overlapping fleshy leaves grow in rosettes from 2 to 30 inches tall. Hen and chicks (*Echeveria elegans*) has tight grayish white rosettes, pink-and-yellow flowers in spring. *E. setosa* has red flowers and dark green, 4-inch-wide rosettes covered with stiff white hairs.

Kalanchoe
Felt plant, kalanchoe

Reaching 3 to 5 feet, *Kalanchoe beharensis* (felt plant) has furry, triangular leaves, crimped at the edges. *K. blossfeldiana* (kalanchoe) has flowers of red, yellow, salmon, pink, or orange; it's usually under 2 feet tall. Tolerates partial shade.

Opuntia
Beaver tail, cholla, prickly pear

Large group includes 2 to 8-foot plants. *Opuntia* divides into two subgroups—plants with flat, broad stems and those with cylindrical stems. Flowers are pale green, yellow, or white marked with lavender.

Schlumbergera
Christmas cactus, Thanksgiving cactus

Spineless green stems, made up of many flat segments, may eventually arch to 3 feet across. Mature plants produce tubular flowers in white, pink, salmon, and rosy red; some colors look almost fluorescent.

Sempervivum tectorum
Hen and chickens

Rosettes of leaves with reddish brown, bristle-pointed tips grow from 8 to 24 inches tall.

Vegetables

Container cultivation is hardly a traditional method for growing most vegetables. But as more and more gardeners are discovering, containers can pamper many vegetables just as successfully as spacious traditional kitchen gardens.

Most vegetables are annuals: they grow and produce at a fast clip during a single season, requiring a constant supply of moisture and nutrients to fuel their work. They also need plenty of room, so be sure to choose containers large enough to accommodate plants comfortably when they reach full size (see individual entries and page 84 for help).

Use plastic pipe to irrigate half barrel.

Plant vegetables in a lightweight potting soil mix. The packaged variety sold at nurseries is fine, but you can make your own if you prefer (see page 95). Keep soil moist; never let it dry out so much that plants wilt. You may want to invest in a customized, automatic watering system—for example, plastic pipe can be connected to reach a number of semipermanent containers (see drawing above). A drip irrigation system (see page 99) or pipe system combined with a timer can make watering all but effortless.

Starting 2 weeks after planting, apply a complete fertilizer once or twice a month until harvest tapers off. (Timed-release fertilizer can be applied less often; follow package directions.) Give your vegetables ample sun—with a few exceptions, all need at least 6 hours of sunshine daily.

It's usually easiest to start with nursery transplants; you won't have to thin seedlings (or wait for seeds to sprout). And by starting with transplants rather than seeds, you may be able to harvest a crop up to 3 weeks earlier. Sow seeds directly into containers, following packet directions; thin seedlings as recommended on packet. Always protect young plants from earwigs, snails, and slugs; see page 109 for methods of control.

Some vegetables, though, are available only as seed—special varieties, for example, and certain types such as carrots and beets that are very difficult to transplant.

Beans

Plant green or yellow wax beans, limas, and snap beans when weather warms in midspring. Set out transplants in containers filled with a lightweight potting soil mix, spacing plants 6 inches apart. (Or sow seeds, then thin seedlings when they're 1 to 2 inches tall.) Large containers (see page 84) are suitable for bush-type beans. For pole varieties, use a 1 by 4-foot container with a trellis attached to it.

Soak soil thoroughly before planting seeds. Do not water again until seedlings emerge; then soak thoroughly at frequent intervals. Starting when plants are 4 to 6 inches tall, apply a complete fertilizer monthly until harvest tapers off. (Apply timed-release fertilizer less often, following package directions.) Place in full sun. Beans will be ready to harvest 50 to 90 days after planting seeds.

Beets

Where winters are mild, you can plant beets in autumn. Elsewhere, plant in early spring. Use a straight-sided container that's at least 8 inches deep; a 1-foot-square redwood planter allows sufficient space for 6 to 8 plants.

Fill container with a lightweight potting soil mix; then plant seeds 3 inches apart. (For continuous harvest throughout the season, sow seeds at monthly intervals.) Thin plants to 2 to 3 inches apart when they're 3 inches tall. Keep soil moist, but not soggy. Starting when plants are 4 to 6 inches tall, apply a complete fertilizer monthly until harvest tapers off. (Apply timed-release fertilizer less often, following package directions.)

Beets prefer full sun, but they'll accept partial shade. Harvest roots 45 to 65 days after planting seeds.

Cherry tomatoes

Broccoli

Broccoli is quite easy to grow. But if weather is too hot, it will "bolt"—bloom and go to seed rapidly, without producing a good edible crop.

Set out transplants in spring for a summer crop, or (except in very hot areas) set out transplants or sow seeds in mid to late summer for an autumn crop. Where winters are mild, you can also plant in autumn for a winter or spring crop.

Space plants (or thin seedlings) 1 foot apart. Use a lightweight potting soil mix, and keep it moist, but not soggy. Starting when plants are 4 to 6 inches tall, apply a complete fertilizer once or twice a month until harvest tapers off. (Apply timed-release fertilizer less often, following package directions.) Place in full sun.

Broccoli will be ready to harvest 50 to 100 days after planting. After you harvest the main stalk, side branches will lengthen, producing smaller—but still tasty—clusters.

Midget corn and red Swiss chard

Carrots

Miniature or short varieties of carrots such as 'Tiny Sweet' are best suited to container cultivation. In areas where winters are mild, plant in autumn; elsewhere, plant as soon as weather warms in spring.

Carrots do fine in a lightweight potting soil mix. Sow seeds directly into straight-sided containers at least 8 inches deep (12 to 15 inches deep for standard-size carrots). When tops are 2 inches high, thin plants to 1½ inches apart. For continuous harvest throughout the season, sow seeds every 2 weeks.

Keep soil evenly moist, but not soggy. Starting when plants are 4 to 6 inches tall, apply a complete fertilizer monthly until harvest tapers off. (Apply timed-release fertilizer less often, following package directions.) Carrots like full sun, but they'll also accept partial shade. Roots will be ready to harvest 65 to 75 days after planting seeds.

Swiss chard

Pictured below left

This frost-tolerant vegetable is both nutritive and decorative. Red-stemmed 'Rhubarb', a variety often planted with lettuce or spinach, also mixes compatibly with colorful annuals.

In late summer or early spring, plant seeds or transplants in a large container (see page 84). Allow about three plants per container (thin seedlings accordingly) when they're 1 to 2 inches tall. Use a lightweight potting soil mix, and keep it moist, but not soggy. Starting when plants are 4 to 6 inches tall, apply a complete fertilizer monthly. (Apply timed-release fertilizer less often, following package directions.)

Chard prefers full sun, but will accept partial shade. Harvest 45 to 65 days after planting seeds. To encourage continuous growth, harvest outer leaves only.

Chard is a perennial. Though it may die back to the root crown in winter, it will resume growth with warm spring weather. Flower stalks will form in the second year; cut them off to prolong leaf production.

Midget corn

Pictured at left

Midget corn's diminutive size makes it ideal for container gardening. Both plants and ears are small—stalks reach a height of about 4 feet and bear 4 to 6-inch-long ears.

As soon as weather warms in mid-spring, set out transplants in a large or extra-large container (see page 84)—a half barrel is fine. Space plants 6 to 8 inches apart; for best pollination, group 12 to 20 plants per half barrel. (Or plant seeds 3 inches apart, then thin seedlings when they're 3 inches tall.) For an extended crop, make 3 or 4 more plantings at 2-week intervals.

Use a lightweight potting soil mix, and keep it moist, but not soggy. Starting when plants are 4 to 6 inches tall, apply a complete fertilizer monthly until harvest tapers off. (Apply timed-release fertilizer less often, following package directions.) Place in full sun. Ears will be ready to harvest 60 to 75 days after planting seeds.

Cucumbers

Many varieties of cucumbers are available, both as seeds and as nursery transplants. Some kinds are best eaten fresh, while others are specifically bred for pickling.

After all danger of frost is past, set out transplants of vining types of cucumbers 10 inches apart in a container about 1 foot wide and 4 feet long. Or plant seeds 6 to 8 inches apart, then thin seedlings when they're 1 to 2 inches tall. Plant bush-type cucumbers one to a large container (see page 84).

To save space and keep fruit off the ground, tie vining cucumbers to a support such as the frame suggested for melons (see page 74). They'll require considerable vertical space. If you lack space for a frame or trellis, suspend such dwarf varieties as 'Little Minnie' and 'Patio Pik' in a hanging basket.

Use a lightweight potting soil mix; keep it moist, but not soggy. Underwatering can result in bitter cucumbers.

Starting when plants are 4 to 6 inches tall, apply a complete fertilizer at half the recommended monthly amount every 2 weeks until harvest tapers off. (Apply timed-release fertilizer less often, following package directions.) Place in full sun; harvest 55 to 75 days after planting seeds. Be sure to keep all mature cucumbers picked; just one cucumber left on the vine after ripening will act as a signal to the plant to stop producing flowers and subsequent fruit.

Eggplant

Pictured below

Spectacular purple fruit and equally showy foliage make eggplant an especially attractive choice for a container vegetable garden. Currently popular—and good for smaller containers—is the Japanese eggplant. Its small cylindrical fruits are tender and sweet. Look for such named varieties as 'Ichiban' and 'Japanese'.

In early spring, set out young plants, either purchased from a nursery or started from seed indoors about 8 weeks previously. Plant in a lightweight potting soil mix—one to a large container (see page 84) for standard large-fruited eggplant, one to a 10-inch pot for Japanese eggplant.

Keep soil moist, but not soggy. Starting when plants are 4 to 6 inches tall and continuing until harvest tapers off, apply a complete fertilizer at half the recommended monthly amount every 2 weeks. (Apply timed-release fertilizer less often, following package directions.)

Eggplant needs sun and heat (perhaps reflected from a nearby wall). Fruits will be ripe and ready to pick 60 to 70 days after setting out plants.

Eggplant

Kale

Curly-leafed kales, especially bright-leafed varieties such as 'Dwarf Blue Curled' and 'Dwarf Siberian', make beautiful container edibles. Flowering kale has brightly colored foliage, especially toward the center of the plant.

Where winters are mild, sow seeds in early autumn for a late autumn crop; elsewhere, sow in early spring. A touch of frost sweetens kale's flavor; hot summer sun makes it bitter. Plant in a lightweight potting soil mix. Thin seedlings when they're 3 inches tall, leaving about two or three plants in a large container (see page 84), five in a 1 by 4-foot box. (Or set out transplants accordingly.)

Keep soil moist, but not soggy. Starting when plants are 4 to 6 inches tall and continuing until harvest tapers off, apply a complete fertilizer at half the recommended monthly amount every 2 weeks. (Apply timed-release fertilizer less often, following package directions.)

Kale prefers full sun, but will accept partial shade. Harvest begins 60 to 70 days after planting seeds; encourage continuous growth by harvesting only outside leaves.

Lettuce

Pictured at right

Easy to grow and attractive, lettuce does well in window boxes (pages 18 to 19) and all types of large pots. For a handy supply of salad ingredients, stagger romaine and butter lettuce with green onions and radishes.

Set out transplants or sow seeds in early spring, again in late summer, and in early autumn. Where winters are frost free, plant or sow from autumn through midspring. Allow one or two plants to a medium-size container, four to six plants to a large

container (see page 84) or a 1 by 4-foot box. (Thin seedlings accordingly when they're 3 inches tall.) Be sure container is at least 12 inches deep.

Use a lightweight potting soil mix, and keep it moist, but not soggy. Starting when plants are 4 to 6 inches tall, keep new leaves coming by applying a complete fertilizer at half the recommended monthly amount every 2 weeks. (Apply timed-release fertilizer less often, following package directions.) Place in full sun during cool weather; otherwise, give partial shade. Leaves will be ready to harvest 40 to 90 days after planting seeds.

Melons

Many gardeners, assuming that melons demand enormous quantities of garden space, have never tried them in pots. Actually, they often grow very well in a good-size container—maybe even better than in the open ground. An optimum spot for the container is against a south-facing wall or fence where the plants can soak up the reflected light and heat they need.

'Great Lakes' and red leaf lettuce

One good container variety among the miniature and bush melons is the cantaloupe 'Minnesota Midget'. You'll need a container that allows about 14 by 14 inches per melon clump.

In late spring, set out transplants or sow seeds in containers filled with a lightweight potting soil mix. You can grow six to eight plants in a 1 by 4-foot box if you provide support or trellis; otherwise, allow just two or three plants per box.

To make a support for growing vines, attach a galvanized welded-wire screen to the sides and back of the container. Choose screen with 2 by 4-inch mesh. To allow sun and air to reach all around fruits as they ripen, hold them up to the light with stretchy slings (discarded pantyhose work well) attached to the wire.

Keep soil moist, but not soggy. Starting when plants are 4 to 6 inches tall and continuing until harvest tapers off, apply a complete fertilizer at half the recommended monthly amount every 2 weeks. (Apply timed-release fertilizer less often, following package directions.) Place in full sun. Melons are ripe when they pull away easily from the stems—the "full slip" stage. Ripening occurs within 70 to 115 days after planting seeds, depending on type of melon and climate.

Green onions, scallions

Small green bunching onions, or scallions, sprout readily from seed sown in cool soil. Or grow scallions from onion sets planted 1 to 2 inches deep, about 2 inches apart, in a planter at least 8 inches deep.

Whether you're starting from sets or seed, plant scallions in autumn (where winters are mild) or early spring in a lightweight potting soil mix. Thin plants to 1 to 2 inches apart when they're 3 to 4 inches tall.

Keep soil moist, but not soggy. Wait until the first warmth of spring before fertilizing autumn-planted scallions. Otherwise, starting 1 month from planting, apply a complete fertilizer at half the recommended monthly amount every 2 weeks. (Or apply timed-release fertilizer as package directs.) Give scallions full sun or partial shade. They usually take 2 to 3 months to reach usable size.

Peppers

Peppers make near-perfect container plants: attractive to look at, they also provide a plentiful, sustained crop. Set out transplants of either sweet or hot varieties, one or two to a large container (see page 84), when weather warms in spring. (Or sow seeds, then thin seedlings when they're 1 to 2 inches tall.)

Use a lightweight potting soil mix, and keep it moist, but not soggy. Allowing soil to dry out slightly between waterings late in the season (early autumn) speeds maturity.

Starting when plants are 4 to 6 inches tall and continuing until harvest tapers off, apply a complete fertilizer at half the recommended monthly amount every 2 weeks. (Apply timed-release fertilizer less often, following package directions.) Locate in full sun. You can begin harvesting peppers 60 to 80 days after planting seeds.

Radishes

Fast-growing and diminutive, radishes will thrive in any container that's 8 or more inches deep. Try combining them in a large wooden planter with other cool-weather vegetables such as carrots, lettuce, and beets.

Where winters are mild, plant all year; elsewhere, plant in spring or autumn. Sow seeds directly into containers filled with a lightweight potting soil mix. Planting a few more seeds every 2 weeks will ensure a continuous crop. When seedlings are 1 to 2 inches tall, thin to 1 to 4 inches apart.

Keep soil moist, but not soggy; fertilize sparingly. Place in either full sun or partial shade. Roots will be ready to harvest 22 to 70 days after planting seeds.

Squash

Pictured at left

For a container, select high-yielding, fast-growing bush forms of summer squash, such as 'Early Summer Crookneck' or 'Aristocrat' zucchini. Big, lush plants, they require heavy watering and fertilizing.

In spring, set out transplants or plant seeds in a lightweight potting soil mix, allowing one plant to a large container (see page 84). Thin seedlings accordingly when they're 1 to 2 inches tall. Keep soil moist, but not soggy. Starting when plants are 4 to 6 inches tall and continuing until harvest tapers off, apply a complete fertilizer at half the recommended monthly amount every 2 weeks. (Apply timed-release fertilizer less often, following package directions.)

Squash need full sun. Fruits will be ready to pick 50 to 60 days after planting seeds. Continuous harvesting prolongs production.

Winter squash require the same care, but take longer to ripen—60 to 110 days.

Tomatoes

Pictured on page 72

Tasty, easy-to-grow tomatoes offer numerous varieties that thrive in a sun-soaked container. Medium-size and cherry-type tomatoes are good for pots; suitable varieties include 'Dwarf Champion', 'Early Salad', 'Patio Hybrid', 'Presto', and (all cherry size) 'Pixie', 'Small Fry', 'Sugar Lump', 'Tiny Tim', and 'Tumblin' Tom'. Grow these in a medium-size container (see page 84) or hanging basket.

You can grow heavier tomatoes in pots, too; they require a large container (see page 84) plus some support, such as a large-mesh wire cage similar to that used for melons (see facing page). Big, delicious choices include 'Big Boy', 'Beefmaster', and 'Beefeater'.

Set out young plants in mid-spring, one to a container. You can purchase plants from a nursery or start them from seed indoors, 6 to 8 weeks before planting time. Use a lightweight potting soil mix, and keep it moist, but not soggy. Starting when plants are 4 to 6 inches tall and continuing until harvest tapers off, apply a complete fertilizer at half the recommended monthly amount every 2 weeks. (Apply timed-release fertilizer less often, following package directions.)

Place tomatoes in full sun. Fruits will be ripe and ready to pick 55 to 90 days after setting out plants. If an early autumn frost threatens the last of your tomato crop, it's easy to move the container to a protected spot and prolong the harvest.

Tomatoes are susceptible to attack by hornworms and whiteflies. Pick hornworms off plants and squash them, or use a commercial hornworm remedy. For methods of controlling whiteflies, see page 109.

Summer scallop squash

Herbs

Richer in history and folklore than any other group of plants, herbs have been treasured as a source of strength and healing for thousands of years. To many of us, though, these flavorful and fragrant plants are primarily associated with cooking. And when you visit a good cook who's also a gardener, you're likely to find a few pots of herbs basking in a sunny kitchen window or in a bright spot outdoors. A pretty pot or two of herbs—perhaps complete with scissors for easy snipping—makes a pleasing and practical gift for anyone who enjoys cooking (see drawing at left).

Hook scissors on pot for handy herb snipping.

Undemanding and easy to grow, most herbs thrive in containers. (Some, like mint, should be planted in a pot or box to keep their rampant growth within bounds.) Grow herbs in a standard packaged lightweight soil mix. Almost all appreciate an application of a complete fertilizer once or twice a month, from spring through summer. (If you use timed-release fertilizer, you needn't apply it as often; follow package directions.) Herbs usually do best in a sun-soaked location, though a few also accept partial shade. Some herbs are annuals, so need to be replanted each spring. Others are perennials and live from year to year.

Most herbs grow happily in containers between 8 and 12 inches across. Many will do just as well in smaller pots but you'll need to water them more often—the smaller the pot, the faster its soil dries out.

You can start herbs from nursery transplants or from seed. Some herbs are available both ways; others—rosemary, tarragon, and oregano, for example—are sold only or primarily as transplants. Dill is usually sold only as seed. Spring is the best time to set out young plants, but you can buy them from spring through autumn.

You can start harvesting herbs as soon as a good number of leaves appear on young plants. Snip off leaves as you need them, but avoid trimming off more than one-third of the foliage at one time.

Basil

A favorite Italian seasoning, shiny basil leaves have a sharp, spicy flavor that brings out the best in egg, meat, cheese, and tomato dishes. Combine with garlic and oil for pesto sauce.

Set out basil transplants in spring, one to a 4-inch pot or two or three to an 8 to 10-inch pot. (Or sow seeds in pots according to packet directions, then thin (transplant extra seedlings to additional containers). Use a lightweight potting soil mix; keep soil moist, but not soggy. Apply a complete fertilizer at one-fourth the recommended monthly amount every 2 weeks from spring through summer, starting as soon as plants are actively growing. (Apply timed-release fertilizer less often, following package directions.)

Basil does well in either full sun or partial shade. You can start using leaves as soon as they're plentiful.

Pinch off growing tips periodically to encourage growth and give plants a bushy shape.

Chervil

This delicate-flavored annual lends a subtle refinement to such favorite dishes as potato salad and omelets.

In spring, sow seeds thinly over lightweight potting soil mix in an 8 to 9-inch pot. Thin seedlings when they're 1 to 2 inches tall, leaving 4 or 5 plants per pot. (Or set out transplants.) A month later, plant seeds or transplants again in another pot to provide a continuous supply of fresh chervil leaves from spring through autumn.

Keep soil moist, but not soggy. Apply a complete fertilizer at half the recommended monthly amount every 2 weeks from spring through summer, starting as soon as plants are actively growing. (Apply timed-release fertilizer less often, following package directions.) Place containers in partial shade.

You can start using leaves as soon as they're fairly plentiful. To encourage fuller foliage, cut off flower stems when buds form.

Peppermint, thyme, tarragon (left); mint, pineapple mint (top); cilantro, sweet marjoram, sage (right)

Chives

Pictured on page 78

The tubular leaves that rise in grassy clumps from the small bulbs of chives (*Allium schoenoprasum*) have a mild onion flavor. Garlic chives—*Allium tuberosum*—taste mildly of garlic. Both kinds of chives add extra zip to salads and omelets. These perennial plants usually die back in cold-winter areas, then sprout anew in spring.

Chives are usually started from transplants, though they're also easy to grow from seed. Set out plants in spring, one to an 8 to 10-inch pot. Or sow seeds, then thin seedlings when they're 1 to 2 inches tall. Use a lightweight potting soil mix, and keep it moist, but not soggy. Every 2 weeks from spring through summer, apply a complete fertilizer at half the recommended monthly amount, starting when plants are 4 to 6 inches tall. (Apply timed-release fertilizer less often, following package directions.) Place plants in full sun or partial shade. Snip leaves as soon as plants are actively growing.

Chinese parsley, cilantro, coriander

Pictured on facing page

This aromatic, nippy-tasting annual herb is a favorite in Chinese and Mexican cookery. Both seeds (called coriander seeds) and leaves are used as seasoning. You'll often find bunches of the fresh leaves—and the plant itself—labeled as Chinese parsley or cilantro.

Cilantro is not a particularly long-lived plant, so it's best to plant a succession of crops, each one 2 weeks apart.

Set out transplants in spring, one to an 8 to 10-inch pot. Or sow seeds, then thin seedlings when they're 1 to 2 inches tall. Apply a complete fertilizer at half the recommended monthly amount every 2 weeks from spring through summer, starting when plants have 12 or more leaves. (Apply timed-release fertilizer less often, following package directions.) Give cilantro full sun. Start clipping sprigs when plants are 6 inches tall; continue to clip regularly to help keep plants healthy. Harvest seeds when they're ripe.

Dill

Its feathery green leaves and small pale yellow flowers make this favorite annual herb an attractive choice for a patio pot. Use its aromatic leaves and seeds in sauces, breads, and fish, meat, and chicken dishes.

In spring, sow seeds in a lightweight potting soil mix. Thin to 4 to 6 inches apart when plants are 2 inches tall. Keep soil moist, but not soggy. Starting when plants are 4 to 6 inches tall, apply a complete fertilizer at half the recommended monthly amount every 2 weeks. (Apply timed-release fertilizer less often, following package directions.) Stop fertilizer application as soon as flower heads form in summer. Place dill in a bright, sunny spot.

Clip foliage at any time; it's most aromatic just as the flowers are opening. Harvest seeds when they're ripe.

Garlic

You can grow garlic cloves from mother bulbs or sets, sold at many nurseries and garden centers.

Plant the separated unpeeled cloves in spring. Choose a container that's at least 8 inches deep. Fill container with a lightweight potting soil mix; then plant cloves pointed end up, 1 to 2 inches deep and 6 inches apart.

Keep soil moist, but not soggy. Apply a complete fertilizer once a month from spring through summer, starting when plants are 4 to 6 inches tall. (Apply timed-release fertilizer less often, following package directions.) Locate in full sun or partial shade.

When leafy tops begin to droop, harvest bulbs; dry in sun, then clean and store in dry, cool, well-ventilated place.

Marjoram

Pictured on facing page

The small, fuzzy leaves of this 2-foot shrub taste like a sweeter, more delicate version of oregano leaves. Like oregano, marjoram is a perennial—but it's not as cold tolerant, so bring it indoors during freezing weather.

Plant transplants in spring, one to an 8 to 10-inch pot, in a lightweight potting soil mix. Keep soil moist, but not soggy. From spring through autumn, apply a complete fertilizer at half the recommended monthly amount every 2 weeks, starting when plants are 4 to 6 inches tall. (Apply timed-release fertilizer less often, following package directions.) Give marjoram full sun. Start using leaves as soon as they're fairly plentiful.

Mint

Pictured on facing page

This bushy perennial is available in several varieties. The flavor of leaves varies from one kind to another; in addition to the familiar spearmint and peppermint, you'll find apple and orange-flavored types. Mint is perhaps best grown in a container, since it spreads rapidly. Use leaves for a garnish or as a seasoning for lamb, cold drinks, and teas.

Mint tolerates diverse conditions, but for best results, use a lightweight potting soil mix and give plants plenty of water. Plant transplants in spring or summer, one to an 8-inch or larger pot (each plant spreads by runners to fill its pot rapidly). From spring through summer, apply a complete fertilizer once a month, starting when plants are 4 to 6 inches tall. (Apply timed-release fertilizer less often, following package directions.) Place pot in partial shade. Start using leaves as soon as they're fairly plentiful.

Oregano (lower left) and sage (lower right)

Oregano

Pictured on page 77

Oregano is a dependable plant, quite tolerant of cold temperatures. Used both fresh and dried, its leaves provide much of the distinctive flavor of Mexican and Italian cooking.

Set out transplants in spring or summer, one to an 8 to 10-inch pot. Use a lightweight potting soil mix; keep soil moist, but not soggy. Apply a complete fertilizer once a month from spring through summer, starting when plants are 4 to 6 inches tall. (Apply timed-release fertilizer less often, following package directions.) Locate in full sun.

You can start using leaves as soon as they're fairly plentiful. To encourage full, bushy foliage, occasionally cut plants back by about one-third; don't let flower buds form.

Parsley

Use this biennial herb fresh as a garnish, fresh or dried in countless recipes. You can pick its decorative, ferny foliage the year around. Parsley is a good choice for mixed plantings: try combining it with other herbs, or plant it in a large container as a bright green border around colorful annuals or bulbs.

Parsley is commonly available in two forms, usually labeled "curled" (sometimes "triple curled") and "Italian flat leaf." Some feel that the latter form tastes slightly stronger.

Set out parsley transplants in spring, two to an 8 to 10-inch pot, spacing plants 3 inches apart. (Seeds are very slow.) Use a lightweight potting soil mix; keep soil moist, but not soggy. Apply a complete fertilizer once a month from spring through summer, starting when plants are about 4 inches tall. (Apply timed-

release fertilizer less often, following package directions.) Parsley does best in partial shade, but can also be grown in morning-sun-only and full-sun locations. Start clipping sprigs as soon as they're fairly plentiful. Parsley is best replanted each spring.

Rosemary

Pictured on page 29

Use the fresh or dried leaves of this sturdy shrub to season meat and vegetables; branches give barbecue smoke a delicious fragrance.

For a hanging pot or ground-level planter, consider the low-growing, twisting variety called 'Prostratus'. Its glossy, needlelike foliage, bright with tiny lavender blue flowers in winter and spring, spills gracefully over the container.

Plant transplants in spring, one to a 10 to 12-inch pot. Use a lightweight potting soil mix, and allow it to dry out somewhat between waterings. Apply a complete fertilizer once a month from spring through summer, starting when plants are about 4 inches tall. (Apply timed-release fertilizer less often, following package directions.) Keep pot in full sun. You can begin clipping sprigs as soon as they're fairly plentiful.

Sage

Pictured at right and on pages 76, 77

This familiar perennial puts forth narrow gray leaves surrounding spikes of fragrant violet flowers. Variegated forms have leaves tinged with white, purple, gold, or all three colors. Fresh or dried sage leaves lend savory flavor to lamb, poultry, stuffings, and cheese dishes.

Sage does best in a lightweight potting soil mix. Plant transplants in spring, one to an 8 to 10-inch pot.

Let soil dry out somewhat between waterings. Apply a complete fertilizer once a month from spring through summer, starting when plants are about 4 inches tall. (Apply timed-release fertilizer less often, following package directions.) Place in full sun.

You can start using leaves as soon as they're fairly plentiful. Cut back stems after blooming.

Tarragon

Pictured on page 76

Tarragon's dark green, pointed, richly aromatic leaves cluster along woody, spreading branches. The fresh or dried leaves of this perennial add a distinctive flavor to vinegars, fish, egg dishes, and salads.

Plant transplants in spring, one to a 10 to 12-inch pot (plants grown from seed are not true culinary tarragon). Use a lightweight potting soil mix, and keep it moist, but not soggy. Apply a complete fertilizer once a month from spring through summer, starting when plants are 4 to 6 inches tall. (Apply timed-release

fertilizer less often, following package directions.) Where summers are hot and dry, give morning sun only; elsewhere, this herb enjoys full sun all day. Begin harvesting leaves as soon as they're fairly plentiful. Tarragon dies down to the ground in winter.

Thyme

Pictured on page 76

A shrubby perennial, common thyme quickly spreads to 2 feet across if not snipped back frequently. Fresh or dried, its leaves impart a strong, aromatic flavor that enhances meat, vegetable, and poultry dishes.

Plant thyme transplants in spring, one to a 10 to 12-inch pot. Use a lightweight potting soil mix; let soil dry out somewhat between waterings. Apply a complete fertilizer once a month from spring through summer, starting when plants are about 4 inches tall. (Apply timed-release fertilizer less often, following package directions.) Place in full sun.

Start to snip sprigs as soon as foliage fills out.

Golden sage, chives, *Viola wittrockiana* (pansy)

Fruits & berries

Nothing quite surpasses the fresh, sweet flavor of home-grown fruits and berries. Though not every kind of fruit can grow successfully in the limited space of a container, quite a few do very well if given the right growing conditions—including adequate room for their roots. Many of these plants are good candidates for a large planter box or half barrel (see page 84 for information on selecting a container of the appropriate size). Eventually, most fruit trees and berry bushes require a move to a larger home; see pages 96 to 97 for repotting pointers.

Fruit trees make attractive container espalier.

Some fruit trees are naturally small, and thus suitable for containers. In general, though, dwarf varieties are your best bet. These come in two types: genetic and grafted. (Some kinds of fruit trees include both types.) Despite their modest height, all dwarf trees bear full-size fruit.

One of the best ways to grow fruit-bearing plants in containers is to train them as espaliers—with their branches growing in a flat pattern against a wall or fence, on a trellis, or along horizontal wires. (You can even attach a simple wooden trellis directly to a container.) This centuries-old method of training saves space and often increases the crop; it's also highly decorative (see drawing above). See page 105 for further information.

For the most abundant crop, take care to give your plants sufficient water and fertilizer. Keep soil in containers moist; never let it dry out completely between waterings. Unless otherwise noted in the following entries, apply a complete fertilizer monthly from spring through summer. (Timed-release fertilizers can be applied less frequently; follow package directions.)

If you find evidence of pests or diseases (see pages 108 to 109), control the problem at once—before fruit is affected.

With a few exceptions, all kinds of fruits and berries need at least 6 hours of sunshine a day to set, ripen, and sweeten a crop.

Blueberries

Unless you live where soil is naturally acidic (in the northwestern or northeastern United States, for example), container gardening is the best or only way to grow blueberries. These plants require cool, acid soil, lots of water, ample sun, and perfect drainage.

Plant bare-root blueberry bushes in early spring. For best pollination (needed to produce berries) you'll have to plant two varieties. Try 'Berkeley', 'Bluecrop', 'Blueray', 'Coville', 'Dixi', 'Earliblue', or 'Jersey'.

Choose 2 to 3-year-old certified plants that are 1 to 3 feet tall; they'll reach a height of 4 to 5 feet when mature.

Plant each bush in a large container (see page 84). To provide the excellent drainage that these plants need, use a soil substitute of 80 percent acidic organic material such as peat moss. (If you have problems wetting peat moss, use one of the soaplike "wetting agents" sold at nurseries.) Apply fertilizer once a year only, in midspring, using a complete acid fertilizer (see page 102). Prune back long shoots to keep plant looking neat. Place containers in full sun. The sweet berries will be ready to harvest 60 to 80 days after the bushes bloom.

Strawberries

Dwarf apple, apricot, peach, and pear trees

Following a cheerful show of spring blossoms, dwarf fruit trees produce delicious full-size fruit. Some will bear fruit the first year after planting; others take 2 years. In general, genetic dwarfs range from 2 to 6 feet tall, grafted types from 3 to about 9 feet.

Dwarf apple, apricot, peach, and pear trees are suited to container cultivation. You'll find several named varieties of each of these trees; nursery personnel can help you choose the best one for your area. The trees are sold in nursery cans during most of the year, and in bare-root form in late winter and early spring (the best time to plant).

Container-grown fruit trees call for more attentive care than those grown in the open ground. To keep feeder roots from damage, always use an extra-large, thick-walled container (see page 84) that holds at least 2 cubic feet of soil.

Plant your tree in a mix of one-third garden loam, two-thirds lightweight potting soil mix. Avoid extreme fluctuations in temperature and moisture content of soil; always keep soil moist, but not soggy. A mulch—for example, a 3-inch layer of straw—can cut summertime watering needs in half.

Apply a complete fertilizer once a month from spring through summer (apply timed-release fertilizer less often, following package directions). Locate in full sun, away from strong winds and reflected heat.

In winter, protect peach trees from peach leaf curl with two dormant sprayings of Bordeaux mixture or lime sulfur. Dwarf apple trees are susceptible to fireblight, so purchase a fireblight-resistant tree to prevent problems. Control codling moths with ryania, tent caterpillars with malathion or rotenone (spray tents only). See pages 108 and 109 for methods of controlling aphids, powdery mildew, scale, and spider mites.

Dwarf citrus

Pictured below right and on page 11

Dwarf citrus trees give gardeners a high return: glossy evergreen foliage, fragrant blossoms, and juicy, bright-colored fruit. These attractive trees grow from 4 to 10 feet tall. Where winters are mild and frosts few, you can leave them outdoors all year; elsewhere, move indoors during winter to a cool and well-lit room, basement, or greenhouse.

Your climate will determine what kinds of citrus (and even which varieties) you can grow. Here are the most popular types and varieties; nursery personnel can help you choose a tree that's right for your area.

'Nagami' kumquat, growing 3 to 4 feet tall, bears 1-inch orange fruit in autumn.

'Eureka' and 'Lisbon' lemons bear almost all year round.

'Improved Meyer' lemon, another year-round producer, is an easy-to-grow lemon-orange hybrid.

Thorny branches and attractive dark green foliage distinguish 'Bearss' lime. From winter to late spring, it bears seedless yellow limes (you'll be able to harvest some fruit during the rest of the year, as well).

'Dancy' is a mandarin orange variety that ripens around the Christmas season. 'Kinnow', another mandarin, ripens in spring. 'Owari' mandarin orange ripens in late autumn, produces nearly seedless fruit.

'Robertson' is an excellent sweet navel orange for warm-summer regions. It bears heavily in winter. 'Shamouti' is beautiful in form and foliage and bears large seedless oranges in spring.

'Sampson' tangelo, a tangerine–grapefruit hybrid, produces fruit with reddish orange pulp in late winter to early spring. It's excellent for juice and marmalade.

Plant dwarf citrus trees in late winter or early spring. Move each tree from its nursery can into a large or extra-large container (see page 84) filled with a mix of one-third garden loam, two-thirds lightweight potting soil mix. Keep soil moist, but not soggy. Apply a complete citrus-type fertilizer (see page 102) once a month, spring through summer. Locate in full sun or partial shade.

Pineapple guava, strawberry guava

Subtropical pineapple guava (*Feijoa sellowiana*) bears in autumn, producing gray green, mild-tasting fruit with a flavor reminiscent of pineapple. Its handsome leaves are glossy dark green on the upper surface, silvery white beneath. Strawberry guava (*Psidium littorale*) bears sweet-tart red fruit in autumn and winter. Its attractive bark is greenish gray to golden brown in color; leaves are glossy and golden when young, green when mature. Both guavas grow 8 to 10 feet tall and branch almost as wide, making them ideal portable screens. (You can prune the trees to a more compact shape—see pages 104 to 105.)

In winter or early spring, move either kind of guava from its nursery can into a large or extra-large container (see page 84) filled with a mix of two-thirds lightweight potting soil mix, one-third garden loam. Allow soil to dry out slightly between waterings. From spring through summer, apply a complete fertilizer once a month (apply timed-release fertilizer less often, following package directions). Place in full sun.

Dwarf Mandarin orange

Loquat

A charming evergreen for deck or patio, container-grown loquat (*Eriobotrya japonica*) can reach a height of 10 to 15 feet. Given full sun, it grows just as wide as it's tall; placed in a shady spot, it has a more slender shape. In spring and summer, it produces sweet, aromatic orange fruit. Its stoutly veined and netted leaves are glossy deep green above, rust colored and woolly beneath. Loquat prefers a mild climate, but survives freezing temperatures.

In winter or early spring, plant tree in a large or extra-large container (see page 84) filled with a mix of one-third garden loam, two-thirds lightweight potting soil mix. Keep soil moist, but not soggy; from spring through summer, apply a complete fertilizer once a month (apply timed-release fertilizer less often, following package directions). Place in full sun or partial shade.

Pomegranate

Pomegranate trees offer showy orange red flowers in spring, followed by burnished red fruits and golden leaves in autumn. Well-known 'Wonderful' may grow 6 to 8 feet tall. 'Nana', a dense-foliaged ornamental dwarf form, is well suited to containers; it grows just 3 feet tall. It produces small, dry fruit, in smaller quantities than 'Wonderful'.

In winter or early spring, transplant tree from its nursery can into a large or extra-large container (see page 84). Use a mix of one-third garden loam, two-thirds lightweight potting soil mix. Allow soil to dry out somewhat between waterings. From spring through summer, apply a complete fertilizer once a month (apply timed-release fertilizer less often, following package directions). Locate in full sun.

Strawberries

Pictured on page 79

One of nature's loveliest treats, strawberries are easy to grow in a strawberry jar (see page 76 and below) or any large container (see page 84) that's at least 12 inches deep. Always buy one of the newer disease-resistant varieties; 'Sequoia', 'Northwest', 'Tioga', and 'Quinault' are all sturdy plants bearing tasty fruit.

Most varieties fruit in spring; you can usually count on a small harvest the first year after planting, with more fruit in following years. Strawberries need protection where winters are severe; cover plants with straw or move them to a garage or basement.

Early in spring, set out plants 7 to 10 inches apart in a lightweight potting soil mix, with crowns at soil level, roots ¼ inch below. Strawberries like lots of water, but don't let soil get soggy. From spring through autumn, apply a complete fertilizer at half the recommended monthly amount every 2 weeks. (Timed-release fertilizer can be applied less often; follow package directions.) Place in full sun.

Planting a strawberry jar

A strawberry jar has many small side openings that hold suitably small plants such as strawberries, succulents, and herbs (see photo, page 76). At planting time, you'll need a little dexterity to get these small specimens' tiny root systems to set properly. Soak each plant's root ball briefly to rinse off extra soil; then plant, spreading out roots.

For 2 to 3 months after planting, water at each side opening as well as at top of pot. (After this time, you can water at top only.) Keep soil moist, but not soggy.

Give pot a quarter turn each week to foster even growth. For information on fertilizing, see above for strawberries, page 71 for succulents, and pages 76 to 78 for herbs.

1) Fill jar to within 2 inches of top of main opening with a lightweight potting soil mix.

2) Water thoroughly; add handfuls of soil to openings. Water gently at each opening.

3) Set in plants with crowns at soil level; fill in top and side openings, pressing gently.

4) Water again, first at top opening, then pouring gently into each side opening.

All about containers

For every plant, there's a perfect container—choose from many sizes, styles, and materials.

In container gardening, the container is half the picture. And the container might be an antique Chinese urn, a clay flue tile, a rustic cedar box, even a crevice in a piece of volcanic rock. You can use almost anything that holds soil, as long as it meets two basic requirements. First, it must promote good health, providing ample room for roots and excellent drainage (see facing page). Second, and almost as important, it must make the plant it holds look good. Pick the container that best enhances both the plant—its shape, foliage, and flowers—and its ultimate location.

A plant's expected shape at maturity is a good guide for choosing an appropriate container shape. For example, a square box is suitable for a low, bushy azalea (*Rhododendron*), while a tall tub fits a tapering boxwood (*Buxus*). A long, low planter displays flowering annuals to good advantage.

When you select a container, keep in mind just how you are going to use it. Should it be wood, to match your wood deck? Will it be visible, or covered by the plant's foliage? Will you want to move it fairly often? Do you need a formal design, or would something more casual or whimsical be better?

You'll have little trouble finding a container; they're sold everywhere, from nurseries and garden centers to variety stores and art galleries. (You can even build your own containers; see pages 88 to 92.) Cost varies considerably—a recycled whiskey barrel is inexpensive, but a handsome, one-of-a-kind ceramic container will carry a substantial price tag. If you do buy a container in a special design or color, you'll probably be choosing the plant to suit the container rather than the other way around. In this case, it's a good idea to take the container along.

Selecting a container

When you choose containers for your plants, remember that the pots and boxes you select must do more than simply provide adequate room for the roots. Appropriate size is important, of course, but you'll also need to consider each container's porosity and how well it drains. And don't neglect the esthetic end—the right container enhances a plant's appearance (see facing page) as well as helping it stay healthy.

Porosity

Unglazed clay and paper pulp pots, untreated wood boxes, and moss-lined wire baskets are all *porous*—they're made from materials that water and air can easily penetrate. *Nonporous* containers, on the other hand, don't allow free passage of air and moisture. Glazed ceramic and plastic pots and some treated or lined wood boxes fit this category.

Soil in porous containers can dry out quickly, so you'll need to water frequently. The opposite holds true for nonporous containers—the soil tends to retain moisture, so be sure to provide excellent drainage (as explained below) and avoid overwatering.

Drainage

Poor drainage is a common cause of failure in container gardening. Fortunately, it's a problem you can easily avoid by using the right type of potting soil mix (see page 95) and choosing a container that can efficiently drain off any water not absorbed by the soil. It's best to plant in containers with one or more drain holes in the bottom; if you want to use a drainless container, you'll need to adapt it to provide proper drainage.

No drainage hole. You've found the perfect container, but it lacks a drain hole. What to do? The best solution is to drill the hole yourself. For a medium-size container (8 to 12 inches in diameter), one ½-inch hole is sufficient. For an extra-large container such as a half barrel, drill four or five ¾-inch holes. Use an electric or hand drill to bore holes in wood or plastic; for clay (glazed or unglazed) and concrete, use an electric drill with masonry or carbide bits. If a pot's glaze is especially thick, carefully chip through it using a hammer and nail (use *very* light hammer taps) before you begin to drill. Support the pot on a sturdy block of wood; to prevent cracking, drill with a small bit first, then increase the bit size until you reach

the desired hole diameter. Adding a little water from time to time makes drilling easier.

Chip through glaze with a hammer and nail, tapping lightly. Support pot on sturdy block of wood. Finish drain hole with a drill.

If you can't drill a drainage hole, you can provide partial drainage by making a ½ to 1-inch "drainage layer" of equal parts river or quarry sand (not beach sand) and gardening or aquarium charcoal (not barbecue charcoal) in the container. Be very cautious when watering a container with such a drainage layer—it's easy to overwater.

Another alternative is to double pot—to plant in a smaller, draining container that fits inside the one without a drain hole. Double potting is a popular way to "plant" in baskets (to protect the basket, place a rather deep saucer beneath the draining container).

Lift up containers. One easy way to promote good drainage is to lift containers up—put bricks or wood blocks beneath, nail on cleats, or purchase containers with "feet." (Hose washers may be all that's needed beneath containers standing on masonry surfaces.) Water runs freely from such raised containers—and the increased air circulation keeps them drier, preventing water stains on decks and patios and discouraging decay of wood and paper pulp pots. A final advantage: Insect pests are less likely to set up housekeeping beneath them.

Raise container up on washers, blocks, cleats, bricks, or feet to improve drainage, help prevent water stains.

Provide saucers. Raising containers slightly helps keep the surface below from staining; providing drip saucers or trays is even more effective, as long as you're careful to empty saucers. Coat the inside of unglazed clay or other porous saucers with asphalt emulsion or another waterproof paint to prevent seepage.

Containers by size

For more information on the right size container for your plant, see the entries on pages 30 to 81.

Small containers. Up to 8 inches in diameter, depth to fit plant's root system; hold approximately 4 quarts of soil. These containers are for young plants and small types such as dwarf annuals and some succulents. Bonsai (see page 54) require small containers, too; special pots are available for these.

Small containers need plenty of attention: daily watering is almost always the rule. Watch plants carefully for signs of crowding.

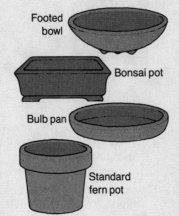

Footed bowl

Bonsai pot

Bulb pan

Standard fern pot

Medium containers. 8 to 12 inches in diameter, depth to fit plant's root system; hold approximately 1 cubic foot of soil. Medium-size containers are suitable for many flowering annuals and perennials, and for some shrubs and vines (several annuals or perennials might be planted together in one medium container—shrubs and vines are most often planted singly). Because of their modest size, you can fit quite a few of these containers on even a small patio or terrace—creating a lot of garden diversity in a little space.

Like small containers, medium-size pots require attentive care. They dry out fairly rapidly, especially after the root system of the plant or plants in the container has grown to fill the soil completely. Daily watering is usually necessary in warm weather.

Standard clay pot with saucer

Glazed clay pot

Plastic pot

Large containers. 12 to 18 inches in diameter, depth to fit plant's root system; hold approximately 1½ cubic feet of soil. Large shrubs, small trees such as Norfolk Island pine (*Araucaria heterophylla*), other trees while they're young, and mass or bouquet-style plantings of annuals or perennials perform successfully in large containers. Daily watering isn't necessary; because they hold a large amount of soil, these containers don't dry out as quickly as smaller pots.

You'll find large containers in clay, plastic, wood, or paper pulp; all are heavy when planted, so be careful where you put them.

Spanish pot

Venetian pot

Mexican pot

Redwood box

Paper pulp pot

Extra-large containers. Over 18 inches in diameter, depth to fit plant's root system; hold 2 or more cubic feet of soil. Extra-large containers are so weighty that they can hardly be called portable—they're essentially permanent design additions to a garden.

Mature small trees such as flowering crabapple (*Malus*) and sweet bay (*Laurus nobilis*) do very well in these containers, as do large shrubs such as oleander (*Nerium oleander*) and English laurel (*Prunus laurocerasus*). Most trees and shrubs look especially attractive when surrounded by base plantings of bright flowers.

Glazed clay Oriental pot

Formal wooden container

Half barrel

Container materials

The all-time favorite plant container is doubtless the unglazed red clay (terra cotta) pot. Lately, though, its popularity has been challenged by containers made from other materials: glazed ceramic, plastic, paper pulp, wood.

If you plan to group many containers together on deck, terrace, or patio, it's best to choose just two or three different kinds. While a group of many different-sized containers of the same kind can be striking, using too many container materials often results in a rather jumbled display.

Clay pots: The all-time favorite containers

Clay pots are available both glazed and unglazed. The two types differ in porosity (see page 83) and appearance, but both come in a wonderful variety of sizes and shapes (many are sold with matching saucers).

Unglazed and glazed clay (ceramic) pots. *Unglazed* clay containers have a natural, understated look that enhances almost any plant and any garden setting. In addition to the familiar red clay pots favored by generations of gardeners, some nurseries and garden centers carry unglazed pots in other earthy tones such as tan, cream, black, and chocolate brown (the color traditionally used for bonsai specimens—see page 54). Unglazed pots have only two disadvantages: 1) they're breakable (see page 86 for directions on repairing them); and 2) because they're porous, they tend to dry out rapidly in warm weather.

Glazed clay containers are often more ornamental than the unglazed type. You'll find them in black, white, and almost every color; some are artfully patterned. These containers are especially well suited to formal settings and indoor use, and they'll give just about any plant a bright, lively look. To avoid clashing colors, make sure the pot harmonizes with the plant it will hold, as well as with its garden setting.

Like unglazed pots, glazed containers are breakable. Rapid drying isn't much of a problem, since the glaze creates a nonporous finish that slows evaporation.

We've listed the most useful and popular kinds of clay containers below. Many of the more ornate ones—strawberry jars, Spanish and Venetian pots—are decorative versions of the basic terra cotta pot. The pots we describe are classified and sold by their top diameter (proportions may differ slightly depending on the manufacturer).

• *Standard pots.* Utilitarian rather than beautiful, these pots are at least as tall as they're wide across the top, and sometimes taller (see drawings under "Medium" on facing page). They're available in 2 to 16-inch sizes; all have wide, heavy rims and either predrilled or knock-out drainage holes. Because they're deep, they provide plenty of room for roots. Use them for relatively tall plants.

• *Standard fern pot* (also called azalea pot or ¾ pot; see drawing under "Small" on facing page). Fern pots are three-quarters as high as they're wide, in better proportion to most plants than regular standards. Available in 4 to 14-inch sizes, they're excellent for azaleas, ferns, and other plants with shallow roots.

• *Venetian pots.* Symmetrical and somewhat formal, Venetian pots are sold in 7½ to 20-inch sizes (see drawing under "Large" on facing page).

• *Spanish and Mexican pots.* These graceful pots, available in 8 to 12-inch sizes, have outward-sloping sides and flaring lips (see drawings under "Large" on facing page). Spanish fern pots in 12 to 18-inch sizes are also available.

Mexican pots look much like Spanish ones, but they're thicker and have a rougher texture. Various designs are often scratched into the sides.

• *Bulb pans, seed pans, saucers.* Bulb or seed pans resemble deep saucers with drainage holes; depth varies slightly, but they're typically less than half as high as wide (see drawing under "Small" on facing page). These containers are available in 6 to 12-inch sizes.

• *Bowls and jars.* Bowl-like and jarlike planters, sometimes equipped with "feet," are available in a variety of sizes and shapes. Some are wide, shallow, and round-bottomed; others are taller, with flaring sides. The pocketed strawberry jar (see photo on page 76 and illustrations on page 81) is one favorite choice.

Concrete and aggregate containers

Cast concrete containers may be either heavily pebbled (aggregate) or smooth sided; concrete "troughs" are especially popular among rock-garden enthusiasts (see page 39). Most of these containers are quite large, so they're very heavy—especially when filled with soil. You may have to drill drainage holes in the bottom.

Wooden tubs, boxes, and barrels

Wooden tubs, boxes, and barrels offer a natural setting for many types of plants, from colorful annuals in a mixed bouquet to good-size shrubs and small trees.

All wooden containers should be water retentive. Check the container's joints closely before you buy—they should fit tightly. Also be sure that the sides and bottom are at least ⅞ inch thick; the thicker the walls, the more slowly heat from the sun can penetrate to dry out the soil.

(Continued on next page)

To promote good drainage and prevent decay, raise wooden containers at least an inch above the surface on which they stand.

Boxes and tubs. Generally speaking, wooden boxes and tubs differ only in shape. A box is square or rectangular; a tub typically has a circular or hexagonal base. Durable woods such as redwood and cedar are widely used in the construction of these containers. They don't really require preservative treatment on the outside, but you should coat the inside with a nontoxic wood preservative such as copper naphthanate (it's green and unpaintable, but inexpensive) or zinc naphthanate (clear, paintable, but expensive and difficult to find). Don't use creosote. You could also try the asphalt emulsion used for sealing pruning cuts. Or use a 4 to 6-mil plastic liner. Punch holes in the liner bottom to match the container's drainage holes, then staple the liner in place.

Half barrels. These containers are typically made from oak. Halves of barrels originally built to hold liquids (wine or whiskey barrels) have thick walls and are less apt to leak than other types of barrels.

To lengthen a half barrel's life, coat the inside with nontoxic wood preservative (don't use creosote) and the hoops with rust deterrent. To hold the hoops in place, nail large-headed nails next to them, nail heads overlapping hoops.

Paper pulp pots

Pulp pots are made of compressed, recycled paper. They are lightweight and comparatively inexpensive; color varies from a sun-bleached gray when the pot is dry to a water-soaked brownish black.

Pulp pots sized 18 inches in diameter and 12 inches deep are excellent containers for vegetables and herbs. Empty or full, they're lighter in weight than other containers of the same size, so they're particularly well suited to places where weight is a consideration.

When kept on surfaces other than soil, pulp pots last about 3 years, sometimes longer. Applying copper or zinc naphthanate will significantly extend their life.

Plastic pots

Plastic pots are versatile and inexpensive, durable yet lightweight. And because they're nonporous, you probably won't need to water too often. Nurseries and garden centers offer a variety of designs, in many sizes and colors. Some containers have built-in saucers; others have predrilled holes for attaching hangers.

Many 1-gallon and 5-gallon plants come in plastic containers, and some gardeners choose not to transplant these. They disguise the plastic pot by slipping it into a larger, more decorative container, or sink the pot right along with the plant into a soil-filled container of greater size.

Repairing a broken clay pot

A broken clay pot doesn't have to share the fate that befell Humpty Dumpty. You can quickly put most damaged pots, both glazed and unglazed, right back together again. Of course, you probably won't be able to salvage one that's smashed to smithereens. And some unglazed pots are quite soft; these may crumble when they break, making them hard to repair.

Choose between two types of superstrength mending medium: epoxy glue or fixture adhesive (neoprene mastic). Whichever you use, follow the label directions carefully. Work outdoors or in a very well-ventilated room, and wear disposable plastic gloves to keep glue off your hands.

As you reassemble the broken pot, bind it together to hold it in shape while the glue or adhesive hardens.

Use rope, nylon cord, or wire for big pots, masking tape for small pots. Also scrape off any glue or adhesive that has oozed out of the cracks onto the outside of the container.

After the pot is dry, sandpaper off any dried excess glue—this smooths surfaces and also colors the cracks on unglazed pots.

Epoxy glue comes in a two-part package—one part glue, one part hardener. You'll find smaller packages of two 1-ounce tubes, larger ones of two half-pint cans. The tubes are fine for small jobs, but for bigger tasks (or for repairing a number of small pots), choose the cans.

Thoroughly mix equal parts glue and hardener; then apply to both surfaces of the pot pieces and carefully assemble the pot. The epoxy will turn clear as it dries.

Don't mix more epoxy than you can use in about 45 minutes. When in doubt, underestimate—you'll need less than you think, and it takes some time to coat both surfaces.

Fixture adhesive requires no mixing at all, and it's almost as strong as epoxy. It dries to a tan color.

Tie or tape pot together until glue or adhesive dries.

Hanging containers

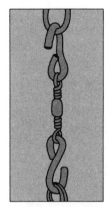
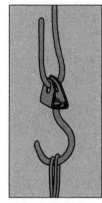

Three swivels: (left) fishing tackle between two hooks; (middle) bent nail, metal plumber's tape on wire hook; (right) hook, swivel, and chain from dog's leash.

Hanging containers make it easy for you to bring overhead beauty to deck, patio, or garden—you can suspend them near a door or window, from an eave or roof beam, even in a tree. Just be sure that the location you choose satisfies the plant's growing requirements (see pages 30 to 81). Also make certain to use a support that can bear the weight of the planted container. Overhanging roof beams, supports for patio structures, and thick, sturdy tree limbs are usually strong enough for most containers (test tree limbs for flexibility before adorning them with plants). Be particularly cautious when suspending pots— especially large ones—from thin roofing or exterior facades that aren't actually part of a building's structural framework.

Some containers are made specifically for hanging; these have holes or hooks in the rim, and may even come equipped with a hanger. Other containers can easily be adapted for overhead use with the addition of a hanger (see examples in drawings below). Use strong galvanized wire or chain for hangers. Hook the hanger over a strong support, or suspend it from sturdy lag-thread clothesline hooks or screw eyes; both are strong enough to bear the container's weight without pulling out of the support.

If you place a plant in a spot where it receives sunlight from just one side, include a swivel in the hanging apparatus so you can turn the plant occasionally (see drawings above).

Hanging containers may be made from clay, plastic, wood, or wire lined with sphagnum moss (see page 23). Where summers are hot, it's best to use wooden, plastic, or glazed ceramic pots; these retain moisture better than the other types.

Moss-lined wire baskets drain freely from the sides and bottom each time they're watered. Avoid hanging these containers above any surface that stains easily or can't be cleaned—or take them down before watering. Other kinds of hanging containers drain only from the bottom; you can suspend a saucer beneath these to catch drips and protect the surface below.

Four types of hanging containers

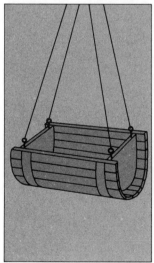
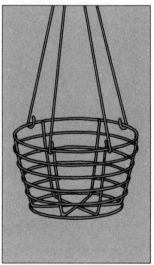

Wooden planter has screw eyes in rim for attaching hangers; others have hooks or holes.

Wire basket's open frame generally ranges from 8 to 18 inches in diameter.

Terra cotta pot has clip-on wire hanger fitted over rim (hanger may slip off smooth surface of glazed pot).

Plastic hanging pot has its own saucer to catch drips. Chain hanger attaches to holes in pot.

Building your own containers

If you've decided to make a container yourself, more than likely the material you've chosen is wood. It's durable and easy to work with, and it adapts easily to a number of different designs.

Heart redwood and cedar are the most widely used woods in container construction; both types resist decay and weather attractively, requiring little or no outside finish. Douglas fir is suitable for very large containers, since it's stronger than redwood and cedar. But because fir tends to discolor, these containers should be stained on the outside to look their best.

Both surfaced and unsurfaced lumber make attractive containers. Unsurfaced lumber has a rough finish, and its actual size is identical to the nominal size—that is, a 2 by 4 measures 2 inches by 4 inches. Surfaced lumber has been milled for a smooth finish. Its actual size is less than the nominal size: a 2 by 4 measures about 1½ inches by 3½ inches. If you substitute one type of lumber for the other in a container project, you may have to adjust the dimensions.

Containers you make yourself can be just about any size or shape. If your needs aren't too specific, you may be interested in making the all-purpose modular boxes described below. But if you'd like a special planter to show off a prized shrub or to complement a particular garden setting, you may want to design your own container (see "Custom-designed containers," on facing page). Here and on the next four pages, you'll find a number of project ideas to spark your creativity, from planter boxes to supports for hanging plants.

Before you begin construction of any project, take a moment to review the pointers below.
- Use lumber that's at least 1 inch thick.
- Assemble boards so the grain runs one way. If boards warp later on, there won't be large gaps between them.
- Glue and nail the corners of boxes; use screws for extra strength. (Always use waterproof glue.)
- Don't use ordinary steel nails and screws. Screws should be galvanized; nails should be noncorrosive (aluminum, copper, or galvanized).
- Paint container interiors with a nontoxic wood preservative (not creosote), or waterproof them with the asphalt emulsion used for sealing pruning cuts. Or add a lining of heavy plastic sheeting; punch holes in the liner bottom to match the container's drain holes, then staple the liner in place.
- Apply a protective outer finish to all containers except those made from redwood or cedar (these woods can be left to weather naturally).

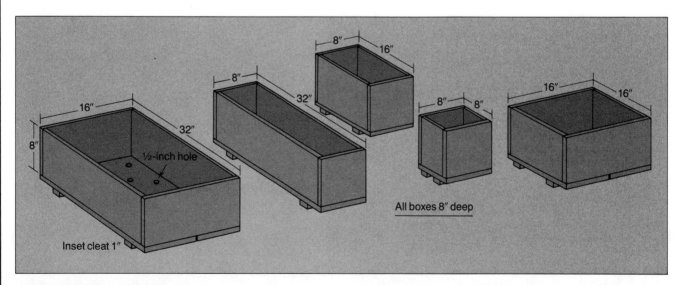

Easy-to-build modular boxes

All sides of these boxes are multiples of 8 inches, making it easy to fit them together in simple geometric patterns. Build the boxes from unsurfaced 1 by 8-inch lumber (use 2 by 8s for larger boxes). Make the cleats from strips of 1 by 2-inch lumber. Cut lumber to the dimensions shown in the drawing. Nail the

box sides together, overlapping them as shown; then glue and nail the bottom to the sides. If the box will be moved frequently, attach the bottom board or boards on the inside of the box so nails driven in through the ends and sides will help support it. Set cleats 1 inch in from the edges. Drill drainage holes in the box bottom—one ½-inch hole to each 64 square inches.

Modular boxes

Modular boxes are attractive when used singly, but they're especially effective in groups. Several boxes of the same size or of different sizes can easily be arranged to form an interesting and harmonious pattern—for example, you can line them up on a paved surface against the foundation of your house to make a bright border of flowers and foliage. If you wish, paint or stain the boxes to match the color of the house or its trim.

Narrow boxes can be used in place of foundation plantings outside and below windows, particularly windows that extend to the floor. You might fill some of the boxes with slow-growing permanent plantings such as boxwood (*Buxus*) or dwarf juniper, and use the rest for a display of seasonal flower color—from bulbs in spring to mixed bouquets of annuals in summer and autumn.

Because narrow boxes take up less space and offer less interference to passing foot traffic than square containers, they're also good for border plantings along paths, at the edges of patios and terraces, or against walls or fences.

Cleated boxes offer several advantages over those without cleats. For one thing, they're easier to move, since even an inch of space between the bottom of a box and the surface on which it stands provides room for a finger-hold. Raising boxes up improves drainage and air circulation, and discourages pests such as sowbugs, slugs, earwigs, and snails from congregating underneath in large numbers.

The addition of cleats improves a container's appearance, too, giving it a finished, furniture-like look.

Custom-designed containers

If you want containers in a particular style or shape, one way to get them is to build them yourself. You can design plant stands, boxes, and tubs to match your house or structures in your garden, or to provide a perfect setting for a special plant or group of plants.

Custom-designed containers can be built to any size. But before you opt for grand proportions, remember that a cubic foot of typical garden soil weighs as much as 100 pounds. If you intend the container to be portable, decide how much weight you can move before you make the final decision on dimensions.

There are really no hard and fast rules regarding proper proportions for wooden containers or the kinds of plants that should be grown in them. But all tubs and boxes look best if proportioned attractively—and of course, they last longest if constructed with care.

Suggested proportions for a low box are as follows: 14, 16, or 18 inches square to a height of 13, 14, or 15 inches. A 7 to 5 ratio of width to height (14 inches wide and 10 inches tall, for example) is also suitable for this type of box.

Pleasing proportions for a tall box are 4 to 3. For example, a 16-inch-tall box would be 12 inches wide.

For boxes up to 18 inches to a side, you can use 1-inch-thick lumber. For larger ones, use 2-inch stock. Make cleats from 1 by 2-inch lumber; nail them across the box bottom about an inch from the outside edges.

Trim adds a professional touch (see page 91), but use it sparingly and keep it in proportion. For example, don't put heavy trim on a box made with 1-inch stock.

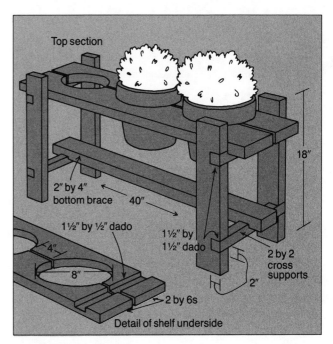

Plant display stand

Lifting plants in clay pots up closer to eye level, this display stand serves as decorative furniture for use on patio, terrace, or deck. Lap joints connect the legs to the top section and the bottom brace, making the unit sturdy enough to bear the weight of filled pots. Leave the bench unglued for easy disassembly; or, if permanence and additional stability are needed, glue and nail all the joints, using waterproof glue and 8d (2½-inch) galvanized finishing nails.

Use surfaced lumber for this project. Cut lumber to the dimensions shown in the drawing. Using a table saw, cut 1½ by 1½-inch dadoes in all four legs to receive the 2 by 2 cross supports. Also cut 1½-inch-wide, ½-inch-deep dadoes in the 2 by 4 bottom brace and in the bottoms of the 2 by 6s for the top section (see drawing).

Fit the cross supports into the dadoes in the legs, making sure the cross supports are flush with the leg outside edges. Fit the dadoes in the bottom brace over the two 2 by 2 lower cross supports.

To complete the top section, lay the 2 by 6s side by side and mark three 8-inch circles, 4 inches apart (see drawing). Cut out the circles with a saber saw. Each hole fits a pot with an 8-inch diameter below the rim. Fit the top section into place.

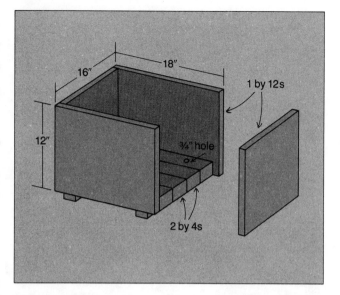

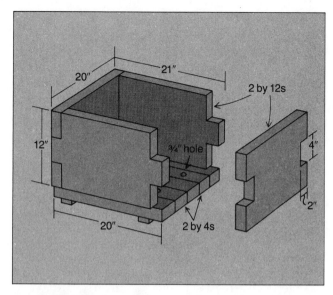

The simplest box

Two sides of this box butt over the other two—typical box construction. Use unsurfaced 1 by 12s for the box sides, 2 by 4s for the bottom. Use 6d (2-inch) galvanized box nails for maximum holding power without danger of splitting the wood. Set cleats an inch or so in from edges. Drill five ¾-inch holes in the bottom of the box for drainage. Position one hole in each corner, and one in the center.

Notched sides fit exactly

The plainest square box gains added interest when the sides are overlapping and notched to fit exactly. Make the sides from 21-inch-long unsurfaced 2 by 12s; cut the notches 4 inches long and 2 inches deep. Make the bottom from five 20-inch-long unsurfaced 2 by 4s. Use 8d (2½-inch) galvanized box nails. Set cleats an inch or so in from edges. Drill five ¾-inch holes in the bottom for drainage.

Take-apart planter

This attractive planter makes a cinch of moving a prize plant to a larger container—just remove the nuts from the four ⁵⁄₁₆-inch galvanized threaded rods and disassemble the sides.

To make the container, cut the following pieces from 1 by 12 unsurfaced redwood or cedar: two 18-inch-long pieces for the long sides, two 12-inch-long pieces for the short sides, and one 12-inch-long piece for the bottom. Cut ¼-inch-deep, 1-inch-wide dadoes in the long sides as shown; one set of dadoes for the short sides to fit into, and one set for the bottom to fit into. Drill four ⅜-inch holes for the rods in each of the long sides and four ¾-inch holes in the bottom for drainage.

Assemble the four sides and the bottom and insert a rod in each pair of holes. Assemble the washers and nuts on the rods, then tighten the nuts, being careful not to tighten them so much that you split the wood.

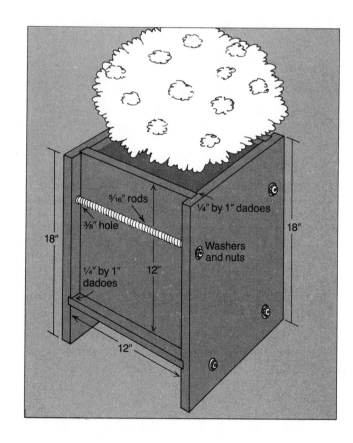

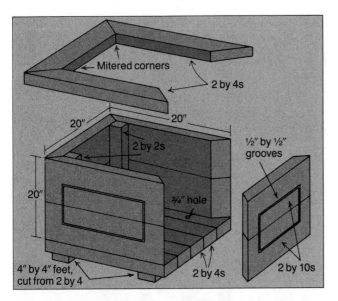

Mitered edges, decorative grooves

Use both waterproof glue and 8d (2½-inch) galvanized finishing nails to hold mitered joints together. Stack surfaced 2 by 10s for the sides, adding 2 by 2s in the inside corners for strength. For a more finished look, add a mitered 2 by 4 cap to the top. Make the grooved design on the sides with a router or a table saw with a dado blade. Nail feet on box bottom about an inch from edges; drill five ¾-inch drainage holes.

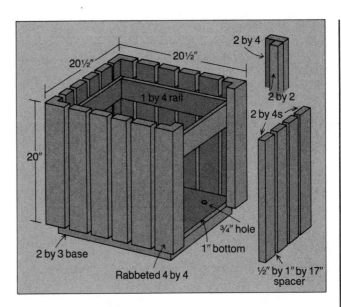

Vertical trim adds interest

Use surfaced lumber except for bottom and base. Make corner posts from rabbeted 4 by 4s, or glue and nail 2 by 4s to 2 by 2s (see drawing). Nail together bottom and base; glue and nail on corner posts, then the 1 by 4 rail. Cut twenty ½ by 1 by 17-inch spacer strips. Evenly space four 2 by 4s and five spacer strips on each side; glue and nail. Drill five ¾-inch holes in the bottom for drainage.

Adding trim to redwood planters

Nurseries and garden centers offer redwood planters in the three basic shapes shown at right. These plain boxes and tubs are ideal subjects for facelifts—you can just decorate the outside with redwood strips. Cut and join the strips as directed at right, tacking them to the container with galvanized finishing nails (drill pilot holes). As a final step, give the finished planter a coat of semitransparent stain to blend the wood tones.

A rectangular planter with straight sides is easiest to remodel. Assemble the outer rectangle on the planter with 1 by 1s, using butt joints. Assemble the inner rectangle with 1 by 1s, using mitered joints. Be sure each rectangle's opposite sides are parallel. Nail heads can be hidden below the surface with a nail set; fill the holes with wood putty.

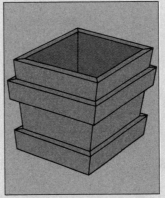

For a square planter with sloping sides, use 1 by 3s. Measure the slope of the sides with a protractor. Consult a compound miter table to determine the exact bevel and miter angles for setting your power saw. Planter dimensions may vary from side to side, so measure and cut each piece separately. Tack on the trim strips with finishing nails.

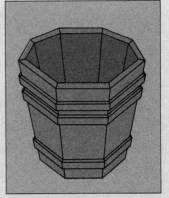

An octagonal planter takes ½ by 1¼-inch strips. To determine miter and bevel settings for your power saw, see directions for the square planter (left). Or use a handsaw, making each piece slightly longer than needed; then file or sand to fit. Measure and fit each segment before going to the next one. Tack on strips with finishing nails.

Cluster of boxes

Four 6 by 10 by 10-inch boxes clustered on the sides of a 6 by 6 post make a good-looking alternative to hanging planters. Make boxes from unsurfaced lumber—backs and fronts from 1 by 6s, sides from 1 by 8s, and bottoms from 1 by 4s. Glue and nail backs and sides together with waterproof glue and 6d (2-inch) galvanized box nails; then glue and nail bottoms in place, driving nails through sides and backs. Decorate each box bottom with nailed-on blocks made from a 1 by 4, 4 by 4, and a 2 by 2.

To mount each box, drill a hole in back and hang box on a nail driven into post. Then slip 6-inch pots of ivy or other trailing plants into boxes. When it's time to water, remove pots to a bathtub or sink and soak them thoroughly.

If you'd prefer not to remove plants for watering, you can drill drain holes in each box bottom where it overhangs decorative 1 by 4 block (be prepared for water marks on boxes and on the post).

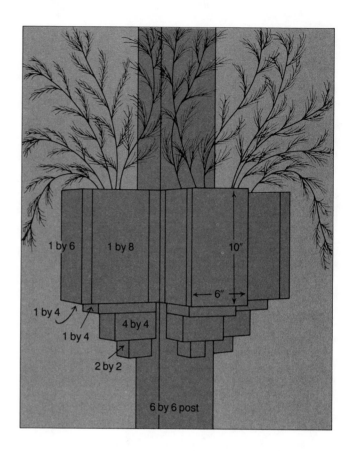

Crisscrossed wood strips

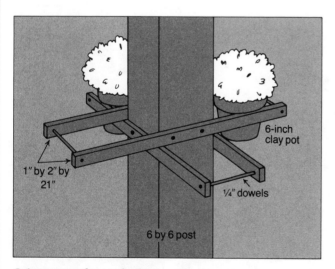

Crisscrossed pairs of wood strips nailed to a 6 by 6 post support four 6-inch clay pots, offering an attractive way to display a small collection of herbs or trailing plants. Each strip is a 21-inch length of unsurfaced 1 by 2-inch lumber. Use 4d (1½-inch) galvanized box nails. Quarter-inch dowels span the ends of the strips to secure the pots (drill holes for the dowels in the ends of the strips).

Hanging plant foursome

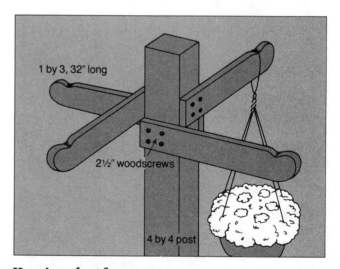

This 4 by 4 post with 1 by 3 crossarms will support four hanging containers. Cut four 32-inch pieces of unsurfaced 1 by 3 for the arms and shape the ends as shown. Secure each arm to the post with four 2½-inch by #12 flathead woodscrews. Hook plant hangers over notches in crossarms. You can adjust length of hangers to suspend plants at the same level, or alternate heights for a whirligig effect.

Moving heavy containers

The first time you bend down to move a good-size container plant, you quickly make two discoveries: the container is usually hard to hold on to, and it's much heavier than you expected. A 12-inch clay pot of petunias can weigh as much as 65 pounds just after watering; a rhododendron in an 18-inch-square box tips the scales at 200 pounds.

Transporting such hefty containers takes a lot less effort if you use some kind of mechanical aid. Whatever method you choose, do the job *before* watering, since soil is much heavier when wet.

Lifting. If you decide simply to lift and carry a container yourself, do it with your back straight to avoid back strain. Let your legs do the bending and most of the lifting. Attaching handles to the container sides or cleats to the bottom makes it much easier to get a good grip.

Sliding. You can drag a heavy planter along quite briskly if you first slip something beneath it to reduce friction. A wide-bladed shovel such as a D-handle coal shovel (see drawing at right) is good for moving containers over grass, ground, or rough surfaces such as exposed aggregate concrete and gravelled walkways. Don't use it on brick, tile, wood, or other surfaces that might scratch.

Another simple slider is a big piece of heavy cardboard (see drawing at right), useful on both rough and smooth surfaces. Open, flatten, and fold a cardboard box; roll or fold over an edge of the cardboard to give a good grip for both hands, then haul away.

Professional movers slide heavy furniture across floors on tough burlap strips. You can apply the same technique to a heavy planter—just place a burlap bag or an old throw rug underneath it, then pull (this method works best on smooth surfaces).

If you're moving a planter from one level to another, use boards as ramps. Tie a strong rope to the planter before moving it carefully up or down the ramp (see drawing at right).

Rollers. Like cardboard and burlap "sliders," rollers (see drawing at right) are useful for transporting containers along smooth surfaces (don't try them on slopes or rough ground). You can use three or four dowels or lengths of 2-inch pipe. As you move the planter along, take up the rollers from behind and place them in front of the container. To round a corner, fan out the rollers.

Wheels. Three or four 2-inch industrial casters mounted on a piece of 1-inch plywood (see drawing at right) make a satisfactory dolly for heavy loads. It may take two people to lift a planter far enough off the ground to slip the dolly underneath.

You can attach some kinds of casters directly to the bottoms of wooden boxes and tubs.

A hand truck with good wheel bearings is another way to move weighty containers (see drawing at right); tie the container against the truck frame with rope. A hand truck is a good investment if you have many heavy containers or rearrange your garden frequently.

Shovel blade supplies smooth sliding surface, reduces friction.

Flatten cardboard carton and fold edge for handle.

Ramp of two 1 by 6s leads down steps; secure box with rope.

Tub rolls on pipes slightly longer than container is wide.

Homemade dolly uses heavy-duty 2-inch industrial casters.

A strong metal hand truck makes a dependable plant carrier.

Container gardening techniques

A well-stocked potting shed holds all the tools and materials you need to plant, water, fertilize, prune, and train.

Many gardeners develop great affection for their potted plants, regarding each azalea, marguerite, or tubbed tomato as if it were a pet with an individual personality. And, like pets, potted plants depend very much upon their owner's loving care.

Though a carefully planted container can sustain a plant in vigorous health for years, it never perfectly duplicates natural conditions. For one thing, a plant growing in the open ground has more options when it comes to getting the nourishment it needs; once it has drawn up all the nearby nutrients and water, its roots may be able to procure more. But when a potted plant uses up its limited supply, things can get desperate in a hurry—one reason why your attention is so important.

In general, potted plants need the same basic care they'd require if growing in a garden flower bed. But because of their restricted circumstances, they demand a little extra diligence in providing the essentials: properly draining soil; adequate fertilizer; enough water, but not too much; the right kind of light; and protection from extreme weather, pests, and diseases.

From types of soil to pest control, this chapter explains and illustrates everything you need to know to tend your container garden. You'll find full details on potting soil mixes, wise watering and fertilizing, and the types of light preferred by different plants; you'll pick up tips on pinching, pruning, and training a plant's growth. And you'll learn how to shelter plants from harsh weather and treat them if pests and diseases attack. Combine this information with the plant care tips given in the individual descriptions on pages 30 to 81, and you're well on your way to a thriving container collection.

Potting soil mix

Many container plants also grow successfully in the open ground, so you might assume it's fine to plant them in the same soil that fills your garden flower beds. But when most garden soil settles in a container, it forms a dense mass that roots can't easily penetrate—and that drains poorly, usually staying too wet for too long after watering. For successful growth, most container plants need the lightweight, fast-draining potting mix described below. In cases where a slightly heavier soil is best (see individual entries on pages 30 to 81), we recommend a mixture of one part good garden loam to one part (or sometimes two parts) potting mix. Garden loam is soil that's rich in organic matter; it doesn't compact easily. If you don't have loam in your yard, buy it from sources listed under "Topsoil" in the Yellow Pages.

Purchased potting soil mix

Excellent potting mix is readily available at nurseries and garden centers. Though composition varies somewhat by brand, good quality mixes always contain an organic component (such as peat moss, rice hulls, compost, or wood byproducts), vermiculite or perlite (expanded mineral elements, popped like popcorn, that help retain moisture by acting like tiny sponges), sand, nutrients, and ground limestone (to keep soil from becoming too acidic). A 2-cubic-foot bag of potting soil mix is sufficient for transplanting 8 to 10 plants from 1-gallon nursery cans to individual 10 to 12-inch pots. The same size bag will more than fill a 36 by 8 by 10-inch planter box.

Mix-your-own potting soil

If you're planning an especially large planting or want a special blend of potting soil (such as acid or extra-light; see below), you'll save money by mixing it yourself.

Our mixes are made with nitrogen-free fertilizer (0-10-10 fertilizer; see page 102), so they can be stored for up to a year. (Nitrogen dissipates more quickly than potassium and phosphorus do—so mixes made with nitrogen-containing fertilizers don't keep their full "nutritional value" for too long.) If you plant during the growing season, add nitrogen in the form of a complete fertilizer about 2 weeks after planting.

You can adjust any of these recipes up or down to make the quantity you need. When you're mixing up a fairly small amount, simply pour the ingredients into a wheelbarrow and mix them thoroughly with your hands or a shovel. If you're making more than a wheelbarrowful, mix as shown in the drawings below.

Store the mix, tightly covered, in a clean, dry container, such as a new garbage can. Dampen it just before filling containers: a handful should hold its shape when squeezed very hard, merely cracking a little.

Basic Lightweight Mix (for large quantity). Suitable for all but acid-loving plants (azalea, camellia, rhododendron, and heather, for example). Two-thirds cubic yard nitrogen-stabilized bark or other organic amendment; ⅓ cubic yard washed 20-grit sand (not beach sand, which contains harmful salts); 6 pounds 0-10-10 dry fertilizer; 10 pounds dolomite or dolomitic limestone.

Extra Lightweight Mix. Often used for hanging baskets and indoor-outdoor plants such as *Ficus* and ferns. Two parts Basic Lightweight Mix (above) to 1 part perlite or vermiculite.

Acid Mix. For azaleas, rhododendrons, camellias, and other acid-loving plants. Four or 5 parts coarse peat moss to 1 part leaf mold. Or use 1 part milled sphagnum peat moss to 1 part fir bark (may be labeled "fir bark mulch" or "forest humus").

Mixing potting soil

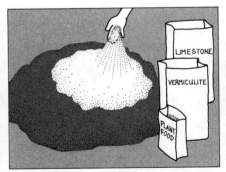

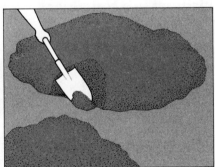

1) Begin mix: Combine sand and organic material in a large pile, then toss into second pile to mix. Toss again if necessary.

2) Scatter fertilizer and limestone over blended organic material and sand. For a lighter mix, add perlite or vermiculite.

3) Toss again once or twice to blend all ingredients. If you're making only a small quantity, mix ingredients with your hands.

Planting & repotting

Methods of planting (and transplanting) in a container are just about the same for every plant, whether you bring it home in a cell pack, flat, one-gallon can, or five-gallon can.

If you're starting from seeds rather than nursery plants, just follow packet directions. Sow seeds in the container you'll use for display, or transplant seedlings when they're a few inches tall.

To plant bulbs, see page 46 for general information, pages 47 to 50 for comments on individual plants.

Step-by-step potting

Besides a container, you'll need a square of metal fine-mesh screen or several pot shards to cover the drainage hole; potting soil mix (see page 95); plenty of water; and a stake or trellis if needed. Also have on hand a trowel and a knife or fork for loosening matted roots.

Prepare the container. When planting in a pot that's been used before, begin by scrubbing it out with a brush and hot water to clean away any pests or disease it may have harbored. Bleach will eliminate moss and diseases; vinegar will dissolve accumulated salts. Unglazed red clay pots must be soaked in water before you plant—otherwise, the clay will absorb moisture from the root ball.

Cover the drainage hole with the screen, then the pot shards (see drawing 1 below). This prevents clogging, soil loss during watering, and entry of insect pests. (If your container lacks a drainage hole, some special steps are necessary; see page 83.)

Remove from nursery container. Before taking a plant from any nursery container, water the soil thoroughly—moist soil clings to roots, helping to hold the root ball together. Always try to leave as much soil around roots as possible.

Remove individual soil blocks from flats or tray packs as you'd lift brownies from a pan, using a knife or spatula. Plants in plastic cell packs slide out easily if you carefully turn the pack upside down and push on the cell bottom.

To free a plant from a small pot, first run a table knife around the pot's inside edge. Then invert the pot and tap it gently to loosen the plant. Let the plant drop out, steadying the root ball with one hand and holding the stem between two fingers (see drawing 2 below).

It's safest to let nursery personnel cut gallon-size and larger metal cans, since the cut edges are treacherously sharp. If you cut cans at home, use tin snips—and be extremely careful. To remove the plant, turn the can on its side; gently loosen plant and pull it free. Because soil in a cut container won't retain enough water to keep roots moist, always plant as soon as possible.

Plants in plastic containers will slide out easily without cutting the can, provided the root ball is moist.

Check roots. If the plant is rootbound (potbound), with roots tightly twined around the root ball surface, score the roots lightly with a sharp knife. Then loosen roots gently with your fingers (see drawing on page 31).

Add potting soil mix. Start with moistened potting soil mix—it should be damp enough to form a ball when squeezed, but not dripping wet. Pour a cushion of soil mix into the container, making it thick enough to hold the top (or crown) of the root ball about 1 inch below the pot's rim (see drawing 3 below). Fill in more moist soil mix around the plant's sides; press it in firmly to plug any air pockets, but don't pack it densely.

Water thoroughly. After planting, set small pots in a pan of water and let stand until soil surface becomes moist. Gently water larger containers from the top until water runs out the drainage holes (see drawing 4 below). If the water passes through quite rapidly, tamp the soil to

Planting in a container

1) Cover hole with screen and shards, concave sides down.

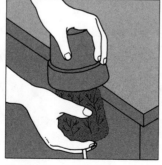

2) Gently tap rim of inverted pot; plant slides out.

3) Position plant crown on soil cushion, 1 inch below rim.

4) Water gently until water drains out pot bottom.

firm it; if the water sits on top, loosen soil with a sharp, slender stick. If the container lacks a drainage hole, just add water equal to one-quarter of the total soil volume. For the first week or two after planting, set containers in a spot that's well protected from hot sun and wind.

Paper pulp pots, burlap wrapping

If you bring your plant home in a paper pulp pot, you can remove it following the directions for metal or plastic cans (see facing page). Or just punch scattered 2-inch holes into the pot's thick paper sides; then place the plant, pot and all, in its new container, and fill in around the sides with potting soil mix. When the level of soil outside the pulp pot is even with the plant's crown, cut or tear the pulp-pot rim down to the soil surface.

When the plant comes home wrapped in burlap, first remove the twine. Then fold back and trim away the upper edge, leaving the root ball covered. Continue planting as directed on the facing page.

Both paper pulp pots and burlap eventually decompose into the potting soil mix without harming the plant (be sure "burlap" is not made of plastic).

Bare-root plants

In late winter or early spring, nurseries often sell deciduous plants such as roses and fruit trees in bare-root condition. Bare-root trees and shrubs usually grow faster and cost considerably less than those set out from nursery cans in the warmer months.

Always choose bare-root plants with fresh, plump roots. (Soaking overnight in water before planting may revive slightly dried roots, but there's no cure for really withered ones.) In many cases, tops and roots should be pruned (see drawing below left). Ask the nursery staff if such pruning has been done; see also *Sunset's Pruning Handbook*.

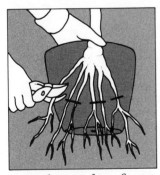

Pruned roots of rose fit over soil in container.

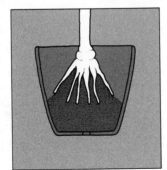

Bud union (bulge on stem above roots) should be level with rim.

To plant, mound soil in the bottom of the container. Then position the bare roots over the soil (see drawing above right), keeping the plant's crown level with the container rim. Finish planting as directed on the facing page.

Repotting

When roots poke through a pot's drainage hole or look matted around the root ball (gently knock plant from pot to check), it's usually time to repot. Most plants need repotting every 2 to 3 years; a few, though, perform best if somewhat potbound, so can go longer between moves. Repot in late winter or very early spring, when plants are dormant.

To remove plants from small and medium-size containers, see directions on the facing page. If you're dealing with a large tub, first let its soil dry slightly; then lay the container on its side, tap around its rim with a mallet, and gently pull the plant free, holding it by the stem or trunk. (You may need to cushion the tub's rim with a cloth so it won't be dented or nicked.) Or float the root ball out by forcing water from a hose through the drainage hole.

You can repot either in the plant's original container (see "Back in the same pot," below) or in a new and somewhat bigger one. If returned to the same pot, the plant will maintain the size it had before repotting.

New & bigger

Never move any plant to a container that's many times bigger than the original pot. Especially in wet, cold climates, plants sitting in too great an expanse of damp soil run the risk of root rot. If you want to give a plant a larger home, it's safest to shift it to a container just one size up. Fast-growing plants are an exception; they can move up two sizes, from a 4 to 6-inch pot, for example.

To repot, follow the planting directions on the facing page.

Back in the same pot

After removing the plant from its pot, carefully pull one-quarter or less of the old potting soil (and any debris) away from the sides of the root ball. If the root ball looks matted, shave it on all sides, cutting off ¼-inch or thicker slices with a sharp knife (see drawing below).

Before repotting in same container, shave root ball if needed, slicing ¼ inch or more off all sides with sharp knife.

Next, score the root ball from top to bottom with the knife; gently run your fingers through the cuts to fray the roots outward.

Scrub the original container with a brush and hot water. Then follow the planting directions on the facing page.

Watering

Because their roots can reach deep into the surrounding soil, plants growing in the open ground may survive some amount of drought. But container plants have only the soil in their pots to draw from; they depend largely on you for the moisture they need. In general, they'll require more frequent watering than plants in garden flower beds and borders.

When to water?

In the entries on pages 30 to 81, you'll find specific information on water requirements for a number of plants. Some need soil that's kept constantly moist, but not soggy—it should feel barely damp, like a squeezed-out sponge. Others fare best if soil is allowed to dry out somewhat between one watering and the next; in these cases, don't give water until soil in the top half of the pot feels dry. Still other plants need even less water; you can let the soil dry out almost to the bottom of the pot between waterings (though not so much that the soil mass begins to pull away from the container sides). Lighter soil mixes dry out faster than heavier ones. If you find your soil mix is difficult to wet, apply one of the wetting agents available at nurseries and garden centers.

After a while, you'll probably develop a watering plan that suits your container collection. Even so, stay flexible: check containers periodically and water plants according to their day-to-day needs, not by a set schedule. During hot, dry, or windy weather, actively growing plants may need watering several times a day. But in cool, still, overcast conditions, you may get by with much less frequent watering. Remember, though, that plants still need some water in chilly or cloudy spells. And don't neglect pots under eaves or overhangs in rainy weather; if no rainfall reaches them, these plants can suffer from drought even during a season of daily downpours.

How much water?

Give each plant enough water to moisten the entire containerful of soil, not just the top few inches. You'll know the soil is saturated when excess water runs freely from the drainage hole.

Sometimes, a container doesn't have a drainage hole. Or a container with a drainage hole doesn't drain after watering—or it drains entirely too fast. Here's what to do in these cases, plus some special instructions for containers with drip saucers.

Container has no drainage hole. When you water a drainless container, add water equal to about one-fourth the total volume of soil (if it's a lightweight soil mix). This is enough to satisfy the plant's needs without leaving any unused water to accumulate at the bottom of the container (and possibly rot roots).

Water not draining. If you've watered a plant thoroughly but no water is draining out, the drainage hole has probably become blocked. Turn the pot on its side and push a pointed stick or large nail into the drainage hole to dislodge the blockage.

Water drains too fast. If water runs out almost as soon as it's added to the pot, check to see if it's simply passing straight down through a crevice between the soil mass and the inside container wall (see drawing below left). Such a crevice arises when the soil mass becomes so dry that it shrinks away from the pot; any water you pour in takes the easiest route out, running around the root ball without penetrating it. To correct the problem, completely submerge the container in a tub of water (see drawing below right). Soak the plant until bubbles stop rising to the surface. If this remedy isn't practical, set a hose near the plant's base, adjust flow to a trickle, and water the soil slowly and thoroughly (this may take up to half an hour).

If water rushes through pot past dry, shrunken root ball (left), submerge container in a tub of water (right) until soil is thoroughly soaked.

Water-filled saucers. If you keep drip saucers under your containers, they'll fill up each time you water (and whenever it rains, if containers are in an unsheltered outdoor spot). Always empty filled saucers within a day; water that's allowed to stand much longer will keep container soil saturated.

Watering devices

How you bring water to your containers depends mostly on the size of your collection and the types of plants it includes. Personal preference makes a difference, too. You may enjoy daily visits to your plants, watering can in hand—or you may prefer the convenience of an automated timed system that tends them while you're away.

The watering can. If you have a faucet close to your containers or if you have just a few containers, the watering can may be your choice. Since a strong flow of water straight from the can nozzle may displace soil and damage roots, be sure to use a can with a "rose"—a sprinkler head that screws onto the end of the nozzle. Some watering cans have extra-long spouts that easily nose in under delicate foliage; use these for plants whose leaves may suffer if they get wet (no "rose" is required).

Garden hoses and hose attachments. To water most container plants, you can simply apply a gentle trickle from the hose to the soil surface. Don't turn on the tap full force unless you've attached a "bubbler" (water breaker) flow head; a jet of water straight from the hose will displace soil (see drawing below).

Strong jet of water from hose may gouge out hole in soil. Slow water flow to a trickle or use bubbler flow head.

Various styles of bubblers are available; you'll find several types that deliver a large amount of water to the soil quickly, yet don't cause displacement. A rigid extender tube that attaches between hose and bubbler can save you steps—it's like an extension of your arm. On-off valves are also convenient, allowing you to conserve water and avoid messy splashing by turning the water off between containers.

One caution: Water from a hose that has been baking in the sun can be hot enough to damage tender roots. Let water run from the hose until it's fairly cool before you begin to water.

Irrigation systems. An irrigation system can make watering essentially effortless, especially when combined with an automated timer. Two systems are particularly suitable for container gardens: drip systems (see below) and custom systems using PVC pipe and standard sprinkler heads (see drawing on page 72). The latter system works best with large (half barrel or larger) containers set in permanent locations.

Drip system kits containing all the necessary components—tubes, emitters, pressure reducers, etc.—are readily available at nurseries and large hardware stores. Most are quite adaptable and can be arranged in a number of configurations. But if your container collection is unusual or extensive, you'll probably want to customize your system with additional components.

The flexible tubes of a drip system can run unobtrusively along a fence, wall, or patio (or even underneath a deck) to reach containers (see drawing below). Emitters drip, bubble, or squirt water to plants at various rates, all relatively slow; select a flow rate that suits your container collection. Use a faster emitter to send lots of water to a large plant such as a tubbed shrub, a slower one to send a gentler stream to a smaller plant, and so on. If the tube leading to a plant is very narrow, an emitter may not be necessary.

Customized drip irrigation system waters each plant slowly and thoroughly. Tubes run unobtrusively to each pot.

Drip systems also require an antisiphon valve (often already built into faucets) and some kind of pressure regulator—either one device at the beginning of the system or a number of pressure-reducing mechanisms built into the emitters themselves.

Most drip systems are equipped with a screen or filter to keep narrow-bore hoses or emitters from clogging. Several times a year, clean the filter and wash out the line. If algae do grow, use diluted swimming-pool chlorine or a commercial inhibitor. Diluted mineral acid (muriatic acid, for example) will remove mineral deposits.

Watering small containers

Small containers dry out quickly, so they need frequent watering—perhaps up to three times a day in hot weather. In fact, people who collect bonsai or other small plants often enjoy doting on them with such patient, careful daily watering. But if you have a large collection or prefer to spend less time with your plants you might want to invest in an irrigation system (see above).

Watering by submersion is another timesaver—during hot spells, at any rate. A good soak can keep soil in small pots moist all day, saving you from repeated visits to containers with hose or watering can. Submersion is also used to revive plants whose soil has become dangerously dry, and in the routine care of certain plants such as bonsai, ferns, and hanging basket subjects.

To submerge a plant, simply lower its pot into a tub of water (see right-hand drawing on facing page) and keep it there until it stops releasing bubbles. Then lift it out and hold it above the tub to drain.

(Continued on next page)

Watering large collections

If you have a large collection of container-grown plants, watering them is bound to be a large task—particularly during summer. To ease things, outfit your hose with a long-handled extender fitted with a bubbler; also add an on-off valve between hose and bubbler to prevent splashing and wasted water as you move from one container to another.

When your collection is especially extensive or if you're frequently called away from home, an automated watering system can save the day for you and your plants. A drip system customized to your collection (see "Irrigation systems," page 99) may be the solution.

Watering hanging plants

Hanging plants demand water more often than plants kept on the ground—and this can mean a lot of work for you, especially during the warmer months. Some gardeners cut this task down to size with an overhead drip irrigation system that sends individual "spaghetti tubes" down into each container (see drawing below left). Such a system can be manually operated or rigged on a time clock for automatic watering.

If you'd rather stick to more traditional watering, at least equip yourself with a long-handled, angled extender fitted with a bubbler (see drawing below center). This makes watering overhead containers much easier, and prevents water from dribbling down your sleeve when you lift the hose high.

If you're going away for a few days, or if one of your basketed plants has become dangerously dry, it's a good idea to soak the soil thoroughly by submerging the plant. Pour water into a large, deep vessel (such as a galvanized washbasin) supported by another pot or a ladder (see drawing below right); then lower the container in all the way and leave it under water until bubbles stop rising.

In hard-water areas

Where water is hard, repeated waterings eventually lead to a build-up of mineral salts in the soil of containers. This residue can harm plants, causing small, disfigured leaves or burned leaf edges. To avoid such damage, leach the soil about once a month: thoroughly flush it with water by letting a hose trickle on the soil surface for 45 minutes to an hour. Or, if it's a manageable size, submerge the container in a tub of water.

If you find you've applied too much fertilizer to a plant, use the same leaching technique to wash out the excess before it can cause trouble.

When pots dry out too fast

In hot, arid climates, it's often difficult to keep containers adequately watered. Try these methods—either singly or in combination—to keep pots from drying out too fast.

Double up. You can enhance water retention considerably simply by putting each container inside another pot that's one size larger. To make this method even more effective, fill the area between the two pots with damp peat moss, then cover the soil surface with a mulch of small pebbles (see drawing below).

Double up pots, filling space between with peat moss. To conserve moisture, further cover moss and soil with mulch of small pebbles.

Easy ways to water hanging plants

Overhead drip system runs along beams, waters plants individually.

Angled extender for garden hose reaches overhead plants easily, accurately.

To protect trailing branches, set basin on overturned pot; then submerge plant.

Repot. A rootbound (potbound) plant—with roots constricted by the size of its pot—has no reserve of moist soil outside the root area. Move the plant into a container just one size larger (see drawing below). Too much soil around the roots can lead to root rot.

Moving rootbound plant to pot one size up will give it a reserve of moist soil.

Mulch. In almost all climates, some type of mulch—pebbles, bark, or a ground cover such as Irish moss, baby's tears, or ajuga—appreciably slows the evaporation of water from the soil. The drawing on the facing page illustrates a pebble mulch; the photo on page 80 shows a ground cover mulch.

Change container types. A switch to a container made from a less porous material can help keep soil moist longer. From most to least water retentive, here's how popular containers compare:

1) plastic
2) metal
3) concrete
4) glazed ceramic
5) wood
6) unglazed red clay
7) paper pulp
8) pressed peat
9) wire lined with sphagnum moss

Plants in pressed peat pots or wire baskets obviously run the greatest risk of dehydration.

Cluster. Grouping pots close together also helps prevent rapid drying. Each container in the cluster shades and cools the sides of its neighbors, and provides a barrier that lessens the drying effects of wind.

Vacation watering

How long can your plants live without you? The answer may be as unpredictable as the weather. So even if you're going away for just a few days, be sure to secure a reliable friend or neighbor to tend your containers. Provide precise instructions telling when and what to water, and how much water to give; leave a hose nearby with the right nozzle attached. To make a sitter's job easier—and for the good of your plants—group all containers together in a shady spot sheltered from wind (see drawing below left). If there's no place in your yard that fits this description, you can build a roofed, four-walled shelter of saran shade cloth or similar lightweight screening.

What if you can't find a plant sitter? You might try placing pots in a trench, then filling the trench with wet sawdust or peat (see drawing below center). Some gardeners bury pots directly in ground that receives regular water from an automatic sprinkler system. Indoor-outdoor plants usually get along quite nicely for 10 days or so if placed on porous bricks (½ to 2 inches thick) in a bathtub or sink filled with enough water to cover bricks halfway.

If you're leaving your plants outdoors and above ground (in a shady spot, of course), try watering them with the special nylon wicks available at nurseries and garden centers. (If you wish, make your own wicks from thin cotton clothesline.) Push one end 1 to 2 inches into soil in pot; put the other end into a wide, water-filled reservoir (see drawing below right). This method can keep plants watered for up to a month.

For additional suggestions, see "When pots dry out too fast" (on facing page).

Conserving water while you're away

Tall, spreading tree creates shade and reduces force of wind.

Put plants in a trench, then cover with damp sawdust or peat moss.

Nylon cord wicks absorb water from pan, moisten container plants steadily.

Fertilizers

Plants derive most of their nourishment from the water and soil around their roots. After the nutrients in the immediately surrounding soil have been depleted, a garden plant can get what it needs by reaching out a bit farther. But when a pot plant's nutrients are gone—used up for growth and leached from the soil by repeated waterings—it relies on you to replenish the supply.

As a general rule, give your plants regular doses of fertilizer from spring through summer or autumn, when they're actively growing. Withhold fertilizer in late autumn and winter; growth slows or stops during these cooler months, so plants need fewer nutrients. For more on individual plants' needs, see pages 30 to 81.

If you use a potting soil mix that contains nutrients, you won't have to fertilize until 4 to 6 weeks after planting. But if the soil isn't "enriched," begin fertilizing at once—if you're planting during the growing season. If you plant in late autumn or winter, withhold fertilizer until growth begins in spring.

When using any fertilizer, follow label directions carefully for timing and amounts.

Complete fertilizers

Most commercial fertilizers are "complete," meaning that they include three important main ingredients: nitrogen (N), phosphorus (P), and potassium (K). The ratio of these three ingredients is given on the package label—5-10-10 fertilizer contains five percent N and 10 percent each P and K, for example. High-nitrogen fertilizer, such as 16-10-4, encourages lush growth in foliage plants; high-phosphorus fertilizer (15-30-15, for example) helps flowering plants develop strong roots and prolific bloom.

Special fertilizers

Certain special fertilizers are sold for roses, citrus trees, and acid-loving plants such as azaleas and camellias ("rose food" is specifically for roses, for example). These fertilizers aren't always complete, so check the label carefully before you buy.

To boost springtime blossom of azaleas, rhododendrons, camellias, and a few other flowering shrubs, gardeners often apply a special nitrogen-free formula (label ratio 0-10-10, for example) just after flowering in late spring.

Citrus trees, gardenias, and certain other plants occasionally suffer from an inability to absorb iron or (more rarely) manganese or zinc. The result is a condition called chlorosis, characterized by yellowing leaves with green veins. To alleviate the problem, use a fertilizer that includes chelated minerals (iron, manganese, and zinc), which plants absorb more easily than the nonchelated forms. (Most fertilizers containing chelated iron also include manganese and zinc.)

Liquid, dry & timed-release

Fertilizer comes in several forms (see drawing below)—liquid, dry, and timed-release. The liquid type has real advantages for container gardening: it supplies nutrients immediately rather than releasing them slowly, it's easy to apply, and—if you follow label directions carefully—it never burns foliage. It's also very easily diluted to varying concentrations to suit individual plants' needs. For example, some plants prefer monthly full-strength applications; others do best with bimonthly doses at half strength, or even weekly doses at one-quarter strength. Liquid fertilizer applied through the leaves (foliar feeding) is especially beneficial to container-grown gardenias, camellias, and azaleas.

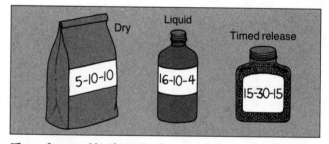

Three forms of fertilizer are shown above, from left to right: dry, liquid, and timed-release capsules. The liquid form offers the most flexibility in caring for container-grown plants.

Both dry and timed-release fertilizers are convenient to use for slow-growing trees and shrubs. These forms release most nutrients over a longer period of time than liquid fertilizers do, so you apply them less often.

When you use dry fertilizer, make sure to water the soil thoroughly both before and after application. Otherwise, the fertilizer may burn the plant's roots or foliage. If the soil starts out quite dry, water very well; then wait until the plant has regained a normal appearance before fertilizing. If you find you've applied too heavy a dose, leach—thoroughly water—the soil as directed on page 100 under "In hard-water areas."

Timed-release capsules go into the potting soil. The nutrients they contain diffuse through the soil a little at a time with each watering. Capsules stay active for varying lengths of time, depending on the length of the growing season, how often you water, and the brand of fertilizer (check label for an estimate).

Sunlight & weather

For the most successful container garden, choose plants that suit the climate, give them the right light, and make sure to provide protection from strong winds, and from intense heat and cold.

Sunlight

All plants need sunlight to survive. But plants, like people, vary widely in their sensitivity to both quantity and intensity of sunlight. In "Favorite plants for containers," pages 30 to 81, you'll find one or two specific exposures listed for each plant—full sun, morning sun only, filtered sun, partial shade, or shade.

Plants that like *full sun* can tolerate really hot, bright conditions—even a sweltering summer heat wave—as long as you give them enough water. In some cases, this intense light and warmth is crucial for flowering or fruiting.

Morning sun only means sunlight during the early part of the day, with protection from hot afternoon rays (particularly in summer). Plants will usually get this exposure if placed on the east or northeast side of a house.

Plants that like *filtered sun* do best in a location receiving about equal proportions of sun and shade: under a tall, lacy tree or an open lath structure, for example. *Partial shade* is similar to filtered sun, but the proportion of shade to sun is greater. You'll find this kind of light under a tightly latticed roof or under a tree with a fairly dense canopy of leaves.

A low-branching, thickly foliaged tree creates the perfect umbrella for plants that need *shade*. The north side of a house is another good spot for shade-lovers.

Chilly conditions

Always shift your container plants to a protected area when frost threatens. Place plants under a tree, an eave, or a porch overhang (see drawing below left), or in an enclosed patio or lanai; the idea is to keep them protected from exposure to open sky.

When a planted container is too heavy to move, cover plant with plastic film (see drawing below center) or a plastic garbage sack, burlap, or newspaper. Use supporting stakes to keep covering off foliage (it draws heat from leaves if it contacts them). Remove covering as soon as temperature rises above freezing.

You can cover smaller plants with a cardboard box. Cut the bottom from the box; then slip it over the plant, top side up (see drawing below right). Keep the lid down at night; raise it to admit sunlight during the day.

If plants freeze before you can come to their rescue, shift them to a cold (but not freezing) lighted garage or basement first thing in the morning, before the sun begins to thaw them. Let plants thaw slowly; then move them to a protected spot outdoors. Don't prune frost-damaged foliage until just before growth begins.

Heat, wind & other extremes

It's almost always best to keep container plants away from a bare fence, stark wall, or other structure that reflects intense heat from the sun. In very hot, dry, or windy weather, move containers under an overhang or shade tree. Be particularly careful to water plants adequately.

Protecting plants from frost

Overhang screens out frost or heat.

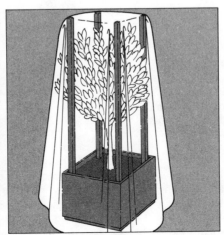
Plastic film holds warmth.

Cardboard box protects against frost.

Pruning & training

Sooner or later, almost every potted plant needs some kind of pruning to reshape or redirect its growth. Pruning also increases the yield and improves the quality of flowers and fruit. And many gardeners apply pruning techniques for special purposes—to train an espalier, for example, or to create a miniature version of a plant normally too big for a patio container.

Basic pruning techniques

For most groups of plants, basic pruning involves some combination of five cutting techniques: pinching, cutting back, shearing, heading back, and thinning. On these two pages, we discuss the general principles of each of these techniques; for detailed guidance on specific plants, consult *Sunset's Pruning Handbook*.

All pruning cuts should be made *just* above some part that will continue to grow: a leaf with a dormant bud at its base, a dormant bud on a leafless stem, or another branch. If you cut into a stem several inches above a growing point, the resulting stub will die, offering an entry point for disease and decay organisms.

It's important that cuts heal as quickly as possible. Clean cuts heal the fastest, so always use sharp tools.

Pinching. Pinching is an easy pruning technique that you can apply when plants are still quite young. With thumb and forefinger, just nip off the tender growing tip (terminal bud) of a branch or stem (see drawing below).

Pinch off growing tips (terminal buds) to force side shoots for a thicker, bushier appearance.

Once this bud is gone, the branch can no longer grow forward—so it puts out side shoots instead, resulting in a plant with a bushier and more compact shape. For annuals and perennials, pinching amounts to routine care; regular pinching keeps woody flowering plants like fuchsia and lantana looking their best, too.

For the thickest foliage, start pinching as soon as terminal buds appear in spring, removing the growing tip from every branch or stem. Then keep pinching as needed throughout the growing season.

Cutting back. For best bloom the following year, many perennials need to be cut back when their last flowers fade in summer or autumn. Perennials having two bloom periods each season should be cut back twice—once after the major show of flowers early in the season, and again after the second, later wave of smaller blooms.

To cut back a plant, use pruning shears to remove one-third to one-half (or sometimes up to two-thirds) the length of each stem (see drawing below).

Cut back stems after flowers fade by ⅓ to ⅔ their length. This prompts best bloom later.

Shearing. Densely foliaged plants, as well as the formal hedges or topiary they often form, need occasional shearing (see drawing below) to keep a tidy shape. On such plants—box (*Buxus*), juniper (*Juniperus*), and privet (*Ligustrum*), for example—buds and branches intermingle so thickly that every clip of hedge shears or hand clippers cuts close to a growing tip. These plants won't be adversely affected by extensive shearing, so you can shear as often as needed throughout the growing season.

Shear plants by clipping branches back with hedge shears to achieve a uniform shape and even surface.

Heading back. A late-winter pruning task, done prior to new spring growth, heading back is a somewhat more precise version of cutting back. To head back (see drawing on facing page), you use pruning shears to cut stems or branches down to a promising side branch or lateral (side branch) bud. The cuts redirect growth in a shapely fashion, at the same time boosting the quality of flowers and fruit.

Annual heading back encourages roses and fruit trees to produce top-quality flowers and fruit, and also improves performance of many other trees and shrubs. Heading back damaged branches helps heal plants.

Head back, just prior to new spring growth, to redirect branches and improve quality of flowers, fruit.

Thinning. Thinning eliminates the entire length of stems and branches (see drawing below). Roses, fruit trees, and berry bushes—and many other shrubs, trees, and vines—perform better if thinned. Thinning improves appearance by opening up the branch structure; it also increases vigor by clearing out old, weak, and unproductive limbs. Like heading back, thinning is done during winter dormancy—once a year or less, depending on how often a plant becomes twiggy or overgrown.

Thin by removing entire branches—to rid plant of weak or damaged wood or to give a more open appearance.

Specialized pruning

Though much pruning is done simply to keep growth in check, gardeners also use certain special techniques to "sculpt" plants into particular shapes. The next sections explain how you can use the five cutting methods just described to train an espalier, topiary, or one of the small "trees" known as "standards." Here, too, you'll find details on special methods of pruning conifers.

Espaliers. Espaliering originated in Europe as an ingenious space-saving method of raising fruit trees. Today, though, espaliers are often trained for purely decorative appeal. Besides apple or pear trees, other trees and shrubs such as bottlebrush (*Callistemon*), camellia, citrus, cotoneaster, and pyracantha make effective espaliers. Brilliant bougainvillea gives a dazzling display, too.

An espalier is trained to grow flat, spreading out along a wide trellis or along guide wires attached to a fence or wall. The basic idea is to direct branches along the wires or trellis according to a preconceived two-dimensional pattern; much of the pruning involves suppressing branches that obscure the design. You can train a formal, symmetrical espalier in a traditional pattern, or choose a more freeform design.

Espaliering demands much work before the full design emerges, sometimes several years of diligent training. Fruit trees are particularly demanding to train: pruning must be done with extreme care to avoid snipping off the plant's fruiting buds or spurs. Smaller decorative shrubs require much less time and trouble.

The drawings below show stages of training a shrub into a formal espalier. For an informal design, follow the plant's natural shape, along with your own sense of artistry. To find out more about espaliering, consult *Sunset's Pruning Handbook*.

(Continued on next page)

Training an espalier

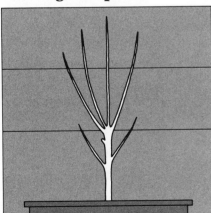

1) Newly planted tree, shrub, or vine rests against horizontal wires or wooden frame. All substantial pruning should be done while plant is dormant.

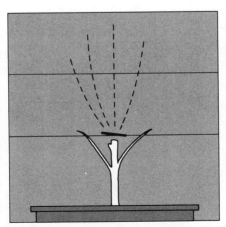

2) Cut back central stem to just above a side shoot. Train first pair of branches along first horizontal support, using noncutting ties from a nursery.

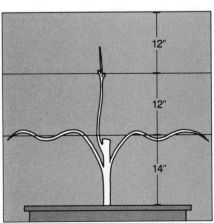

3) When central stem grows past second support, cut back as in step 2. Train second set of branches on middle support. Repeat procedure for third support.

Topiary. In the geometric to fanciful shaping of topiary, pruning becomes horticultural sculpture. To try this specialty, you need imagination, plenty of time, and the proper plants: small-leafed, compact shrubs such as box (*Buxus*), juniper (*Juniperus*), or privet (*Ligustrum*).

While you're training the shrub into the shape you want, use pruning shears to make careful, individual cuts, so you can direct new growth as you desire. Later, usually after several seasons, you can simply shear the shaped foliage as you would a hedge. Easiest to sculpt are geometric shapes like a sphere or cube (see drawing below); animal forms often require skillful bending and wiring of branches to redirect their growth.

Three balls of foliage, rounded by careful pruning, form a symmetrical, geometric topiary.

Standards. When you train a standard, you make a simulated "tree"—with a single bare trunk and a bushy topknot—from a shrub or vine that's normally bushy all over. Floral favorites for standards include azalea (*Rhododendron*), bougainvillea, fuchsia, geranium (*Pelargonium*), India hawthorn (*Raphiolepis indica*), lantana, and rose. A standard hydrangea is pictured on page 17.

The drawings below illustrate steps involved in training a standard. To create a bare, upward-growing trunk, you pinch off or cut off entire side branches rather than just their growing tips. You'll often need to stake the trunk or give it the support of a wire frame, at least in the early stages of growth. When the plant reaches the height you want, you can trim the crown into a round ball—the style that gives standards their nickname, "lollipop trees." If you've trained a vine, just let its stems cascade naturally from the top.

Pruning conifers. To keep your living Christmas tree (see page 67) in plump and pleasing shape, you'll need to prune it a bit differently than you would other plants. As bright green growing tips appear at branch ends, pinch them back or remove them entirely (see drawing below).

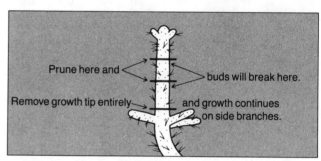

Prune here and ← → buds will break here.

Remove growth tip entirely ← and growth continues on side branches.

Basic control of conifer's size and shape includes pinching off bright green growing tips halfway.

To head back a wayward branch, cut back to a side branch or obvious lateral growth bud. Don't cut back to an area that's totally bare of foliage—no new growth will appear.

To limit height, cut back the central trunk's new growth to the desired height; otherwise, touch the trunk only if it becomes damaged. In this case, stake up one of the next lower branches, training it vertically to form a new trunk. If two leaders start to develop, remove the growing tip of the weaker one.

Training a standard

1) Choose plant with single main stem, full growth for training as standard.

2) Remove side shoots up to 3½ feet above base. Repot into new container.

3) Insert stake, tie stem in several places. Cut plant back after bloom.

Holiday ivy: Christmas wreath & Easter basket

Adaptable English ivy (*Hedera helix*, page 52) willingly wraps around almost any wire form you supply. Try training it into a living wreath for Christmas; for Easter, fashion a leafy basket to fill with cyclamen. Use either project as a centerpiece or an eye-catching room decoration. Make either with small-leafed ivies.

Christmas wreath. If you start your wreath in March, it will be ready in time for Christmas. You'll need two ivy plants in 2-inch pots, pliers, wire cutters, 8-gauge galvanized or aluminum wire, green florist's tape, several rocks, and a tube of waterproof adhesive bonding or caulking compound.

Choose a pot large enough to hold both plants comfortably, such as an 8 to 10-inch pot. The wreath's diameter should measure about two and one-half times the pot height (for example, plan a 20-inch-wide wreath to stand above an 8-inch-high pot). Train vines along the wire—tying with florist's tape, pinching, and trimming as needed.

Easter basket. You can make this handsome basket the day before Easter. You'll need a 6 to 8-inch pot of ivy, its vines already about 2 feet long. (Or substitute smaller ivy plants or rooted cuttings; these will need a few months to fill out and cover the basket.) Also have ready a 12-inch wire basket, a 6-inch plastic pot, an 820-cubic-inch bag of green sphagnum moss, potting soil mix, and hairpins or plant pole pins.

Turn basket upside down and gently hammer bottom to flatten it. Turn upright again; add soaking wet moss to make a 2-inch-thick lining that extends 2 inches above basket rim. Pour 6 cups of moist potting soil mix into center of moss; tamp gently against bottom and sides. Plant and train ivy following the drawings below, then add a pot of cyclamen. During the rest of the year, show off a succession of seasonal flowers.

Twine new growth back into basket; shear lightly, if needed, to control bushiness. You can safely display basket indoors for a few weeks.

Step-by-step Christmas wreath

1) Measure enough wire for wreath, then measure enough extra wire to form a circular anchor in bottom of pot.

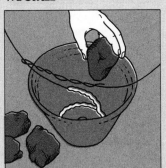

2) Press anchor wire against pot. Apply caulking to wire, then hold wire in place with rocks until caulking is dry (1 to 2 days).

3) Plant ivy in lightweight potting soil mix; water to settle soil around roots. Train vines along wire, tying with florist's tape.

4) By December, ivy fully covers wire wreath. Plants will thrive for several years; foliage will become denser as they mature.

Step-by-step Easter basket

1) Sink plastic pot in center of potting-soil-filled basket, rim 2 inches below top of moss. Halfway fill crevice between pot and moss.

2) Gently divide ivy into 10 to 12 root sections. Plant in crevice between moss and plastic pot; cover roots with soil, then with moss.

3) Wind vines around basket, pinning in place; leave a few free on opposite sides. Push limber 4-foot branch into basket for handle.

4) Wrap free vines around handle. Water basket faithfully, keeping moss moist. For Easter, slip cyclamen into plastic pot.

Pests & diseases

Though many of today's improved plant strains are resistant to diseases, no plant is completely invulnerable to its natural enemies. Life in a container confers no special protection, either. If ants can march from outdoors into a kitchen, they certainly won't be stopped by a low clay pot—nor will snails, whiteflies, or other garden marauders. Below, we describe some common plant pests and diseases, and suggest methods for controlling each one. When you use a chemical remedy, always follow label directions carefully.

Before a pest or disease seriously lays seige to a plant, there are a few things you can do by way of preventive medicine.

• Examine plants—whether newly purchased or established in garden bed or home container—before you pot or repot them. If you find signs of existing pests and diseases, treat as directed under individual listings at right.

• Keep newly acquired plants isolated for 2 weeks so that pests and diseases they may carry don't spread rapidly.

• Always use clean containers, and use sterilized potting soil mix when planting seeds or vegetable transplants. The package label will tell you if the soil is sterile.

• Keep containers clear of weeds, fallen fruit, and dead flowers and leaves.

• Don't try to salvage severely diseased plants; instead, discard them in the garbage. (Don't toss onto a compost heap—you could end up spreading the disease rather than eliminating it.)

• Know your plants and give them the growing conditions they need. Healthy, well-established plants are less likely to attract, and more able to withstand, pests and diseases.

Thwart hungry birds and rodents who like to bury nuts in soft potting soil with this circular screen. Cut hardware cloth to fit the pot's top opening; then add a slit from edge to center, so you can slip the screen around the plant's base.

Diseases

Crown or root rot. Caused by overwatering or poor drainage. Stems (and occasionally leaves) of infected plants turn brown and mushy; entire plant may collapse suddenly. *Remedy:* Correct watering habits and improve drainage. In extreme cases, discard plant.

Damping off. Newly sprouted seedlings develop stem rot near soil surface, then fall over (or seeds don't sprout at all). *Remedy:* Clean containers thoroughly and wipe with bleach before using; sow seeds in sterilized potting soil mix only; use fresh seeds.

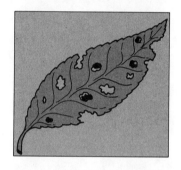

Leaf spot, leaf blight, shot hole. Symptoms are yellow, red, or brown spots on leaves; some spots drop out, leaving holes. *Remedy:* Isolate or discard infected plants; pull off infected leaves, spray plant with benomyl or zineb. Keep pots clean of litter.

Powdery mildew. Usually caused by humidity and poor air circulation. Bluish white dust covers leaves, flower buds; leaves may look curled or distorted. *Remedy:* Move to a well-ventilated area. Remove damaged portions; spray plant with triforine or benomyl (check product labels).

Rust. Yellow or rust colored spores clustered on leaf undersides signal this disease. *Remedy:* Remove infected portions, then treat plant with a product containing folpet, triforine, or zineb to prevent recurrence. (Discard chronically infected plants.)

Pests

Ants. Familiar red and black ants don't attack plants directly—but their nests may harm roots, and some types attract more dangerous pests such as aphids or mealybugs. *Remedy:* Hose off, or use commercial ant stakes, malathion spray, or diazinon granules or liquid.

Scale insects. Hard-shelled, round or oval insects, usually brown or gray. Suck juices from stems and leaves; some secrete shiny, sticky honeydew. *Remedy:* Scrape off or wash off with soapy water (don't use detergent). Horticultural oil is effective and safe on some plants; follow label directions carefully.

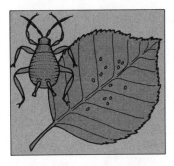

Aphids. Soft, round sucking insects, green or reddish black, cluster on leaf and flower buds. Infestation causes stunted growth, distorted leaves and flowers. *Remedy:* Hose off, or wash plant with soapy water (don't use detergent). Use pyrethrum or rotenone in stubborn cases. Systemics such as dystox are effective.

Snails and slugs. Destructive, very common. Eat leaves at night and on overcast days, leave telltale silvery trails. *Remedy:* Remove by hand and squash, or sprinkle ashes around plant base. Or use bait; mesural forms are most effective, metaldehyde safest.

Earwigs. Brown and hard shelled, with pincers at rear of abdomen. Earwigs attack plants at night, munching on leaves, flowers, and fruit (and on other insects). *Remedy:* Leave rolled-up newspapers out overnight and remove in the morning, remove by hand, or use malathion spray.

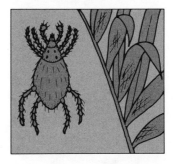

Spider mites. Red or white; show up only in groups. Infested foliage shows a characteristic webbed pattern; leaves may become stippled with yellow or brown dots. *Remedy:* Isolate plants. Wash with soapy water (not detergent) three times, at 10-day intervals. In tough cases, apply sulfur dust, kelthane, or horticultural oil.

Leafhoppers. Small brown or green, fast-moving, hopping insects that suck plant juices, leave a noticeable white stippling on upper surfaces of leaves (though they feed on underside of leaves). *Remedy:* Hose off with strong jet of water, or spray plant with pyrethrum or rotenone.

Thrips. Speck-sized and scurrying, with tan, brown, or black bodies. Thrips feed inside flower buds, so flowers seldom open; also distort and discolor foliage, new shoots. Often fly when disturbed. *Remedy:* Hose off; in stubborn cases apply pyrethrum, rotenone, or malathion.

Mealybugs. Round, white, fuzzy-looking. Typically cluster on leaf stems or at stem bases, sucking plant juices; infestation stunts growth, sometimes even kills plant. *Remedy:* Hose off, wash with soapy water, or touch with denatured alcohol. In severe cases, spray with diazinon or malathion or use horticultural oil.

Whiteflies. Small, white, flying insects that attach to leaf undersides. Foliage turns yellow, acquires a film of shiny, sticky honeydew. *Remedy:* Hose off, or wash plant with soapy water (not detergent) three times, at 10-day intervals. Or apply pyrethrum, rotenone, diazinon, malathion, or horticultural oil.

Index to general subject matter

Index to botanical & common names

Boldface numerals refer to entries in the encyclopedic chapter, "Favorite container plants."